No-Limit Hold'em
Hand by Hand

No-Limit Hold'em Hand by Hand

Learn to Beat the Ultimate Poker Game

NEIL D. MYERS

LYLE STUART

KENSINGTON PUBLISHING CORP.

WWW.KENSINGTONBOOKS.COM

LYLE STUART BOOKS are published by

Kensington Publishing Corp.
850 Third Avenue
New York, NY 10022

Playing cards courtesy U.S. Playing Card Company.

All Kensington titles, imprints, and distributed lines are available at special quantity discounts for bulk purchases for sales promotions, premiums, fund-raising, educational, or institutional use. Special book excerpts or customized printings can also be created to fit specific needs. For details, write or phone the office of the Kensington special sales manager: Kensington Publishing Corp., 850 Third Avenue, New York, NY 10022, attn: Special Sales Department; phone 1-800-221-2647.

First printing: November 2007

10 9 8 7 6 5 4 3 2 1

Printed in the United States of America

ISBN-13: 978-0-8184-0724-6
ISBN-10: 0-8184-0724-7

This book is dedicated to the Crocodile Hunter, Steve Irwin, who was tragically killed in 2006. I have no idea whether Steve Irwin ever played or had any interest in poker but I greatly admire the passion and commitment he had to his life's mission, working with and protecting the interests and habitats of wild animals. He was a completely dedicated and genuine individual who was taken from us in his prime. He lived and breathed his mission and showed us with his enthusiasm and love the importance of preserving the natural world and its creatures. Steve simply made the world a better place.

Poker adds to the enjoyment of life for those who play the game. People like Steve Irwin are amongst those who help to ensure that the world we and successive generations live in is still beautiful and wonderful and waiting for us when we leave the poker table or move away from the computer screen.

I humbly dedicate this work to Steve, his family and colleagues, and all those who carry on his work. From the bottom of my heart, I thank you all.

Contents

Preface: The Rise of Modern No-Limit Hold'em

For those of us who were playing poker at the end of the last century it is still hard to believe its enormous growth to its current status. Sometime around 1997 I found myself sitting around a poker table playing limit Hold'em when one of the regulars, a good player, entered the game all bright-eyed and bushy-tailed. He had recently returned from a meeting of a newly formed group of players who had found each other via an Internet poker discussion forum, and met regularly to play and discuss poker.

"You know, they are trying to clean up poker's image," he informed us sagely.

We looked at each other puzzled: "Who cares about the image of poker degenerates like us?" we were thinking. Then one player voiced our confusion.

"Why?" he said.

"Well, you know," the Sage told us, "for TV."

At that we all fell out laughing (as far as you can fall at a poker table).

"Who would want to watch this?" one detractor guffawed and acknowledging the truth of this sentiment, we guffawed too. After this, every time the Sage entered the room, some wise guy would ask, "So, have you been on TV yet?" and we would laugh again.

A prophet is never acknowledged in his own land and time. The Sage was right and we were wrong; very wrong. Poker is seemingly everywhere now, and it has definitely moved into the fashionable mainstream.

However, the game that I was playing, middle-limit Hold'em, is not the game of fashion. *No-limit* Hold'em is now the glamorous game of choice. Most of what you see on television is either tournament no-limit Hold'em or high-stakes cash no-limit Hold'em. Since these games are often the most thrilling to watch, they make for good TV. It just so happens that, alongside the growth of tournament no-limit Hold'em, there has been another game growing more quietly but barely less prolifically and that is fixed buy-in, small-stakes, no-limit Hold'em. This book is all about making you a better player at that style of poker. So read on if you want to get good and have fun!

Acknowledgments

I would like to thank my editor, Richard Ember, and all the staff at Lyle Stuart for their patience and support. Getting a book out is definitely a team effort. My "home team" includes my wife, Susan, who is always on hand to look over my work and help ensure that my writing is readable and clear. I also wish to thank Alvin Tsang for filming, editing, and producing my DVDs.

I am particularly conscious of the work other poker authors have done in researching, thinking, and writing about no-limit Hold'em. Writing about no-limit Hold'em can be a daunting task at times, as the game can be so complex. I especially want to thank the following authors, whose writings have been an inspiration. David Sklansky, Mason Malmuth, Ed Miller, Bob Ciaffone, Jim Brier, Stewart Reuben, Tony Guerrera, Dan Harrington, Arnold Snyder, and, of course, the Grand Old Man of poker, Doyle Brunson. Without their efforts and insights, I could never have written a book of this kind.

Introduction: How to Join the Ranks of Winning No-Limit Hold'em Players

The Best and Quickest Way to Learn to Play Great No-Limit Hold'em

This book is the second in the *Hand by Hand* series. As such, it is aimed at a similar audience, namely, those who know how to play no-limit Texas Hold'em (the first is about limit Hold'em) and want to improve, fast. As a player, you may have read a number of poker books, and if you are *really* sensible you will have already read my other books. Yes, I am once again plugging my own books in an act of shameless self-promotion! If you've read my book *Limit Hold'em Hand by Hand*, you may notice that I am covering much of the same ground in this Introduction as I did in the Intro of that book, so feel free to skip this section. If you have *not* read that book (shame on you) you will find this Introduction useful. This volume can be considered a sister volume to *Limit Hold'em Hand by Hand*.

So how does one get good at poker? These days there are many good poker books, and I encourage you to read them—no, *study* them—because to become a good player, you must understand the game *theoretically* first. Also, there are many Internet sites where you can practice in free games or low-stakes ones. As I write this, the U.S. government has made an attack on Internet poker, but despite this, poker sites still exist and are populated by thousands of eager players. With an estimated 28 million people playing poker online I don't believe that the United States (or any national authority) can legislate Internet poker out of existence, but the liberty-restricting dinosaurs in Congress will still try, I suppose. I suspect

Internet poker will shrug off this attack, and so I believe that there will still be many opportunities for you to practice your poker on the Internet and enjoy the enormous variety of games on offer across the many excellent poker websites.

This book emphasizes a constant theme, and that is that *your goal in poker is to always make the correct theoretical decision regardless of the outcome of that specific hand.* That is why I never give the "result" of a hand. The result is irrelevant because you cannot control it. All you can control are your own decisions. To play good poker requires a lot of practical experience and you must also have a good theoretical grasp of poker so that you can make sense of, and learn from, your playing experience. Many players improve very slowly (or plateau fairly quickly) in their poker skills because they have no theoretical basis to make sense of what is happening to them in the game.

What is "poker experience"? Playing many, many hands—and this usually means thousands of hours of play. The advent of Internet poker enables you to gain this experience more quickly, but I believe there is an even faster way to learn solid poker. Imagine you were sitting next to a poker expert and could follow that expert's reasoning through a hand. You would, of course, learn about poker theory, but you would also be able to see exactly how that *theory* played out in *practice*. You would be able to confirm your own understanding of how to play your hand by observing and listening to the expert. This is exactly what this book does for you. It takes you through numerous examples of hands in different situations and shows you how poker theory applies to these hands and these situations. Every example illustrates a key theoretical concept and explains it simply and easily. I have restricted the mathematics to a bare minimum, because some players find a lot of poker mathematics incomprehensible. If you want to delve into poker math more fully, a number of other authors have written works of excellent clarity. My favorites are those by King Yao, Matthew Hilger, and Tony Guerrera.

Some poker situations are open to different interpretations, and of course, the human element and the nature of your opposition in any given situation may mean that you occasionally stray from strictly "correct" play. Also, because no-limit Hold'em is such a complex game and decisions are situation dependent, there is often more than one way to play "correctly." I have kept the problems simple so that you can focus on the key elements that the specific problem aims to illustrate. Remember, great poker players are great because they consistently make great decisions, hand after hand. The combination of solid theoretical understanding plus correct practical application in awareness of the specific situational elements equals winning poker. Turning you into a winning player (and a player able to play at increasingly higher stakes) is the aim of this book. If you are still not convinced to crack open your piggy bank and buy the book, here are ten specific things that this book will do for you:

1. **Lessen the monetary cost of poker "experience."** Experience can be expensive, especially in no-limit Hold'em, where your whole stack is on the line every time you enter a pot. Experience usually means making mistakes, and correcting these errors. By studying these examples you will truly learn from others' mistakes for only the cost of the book, not the cost of a pot or your whole stack. You will see and read about correct play in action.

2. **Make learning poker theory simpler.** Learning any theory in isolation from practice is dry and difficult. Instead, in this book, elements of theory are interspersed with practical examples of play. You absorb theory as you learn solid no-limit Hold'em, in much the same way as you absorb grammatical rules while you learn to speak as a child, and not from a book. This will make you a more natural, flexible player.

3. **Teach you to think away from the table.** Poker is a fast-moving game. You rarely have time to make deep theoretical decisions

or perform complex calculations at the table. So how do you handle the many complex decisions you face in the heat of poker battle? Many experts stress that you must do your thinking away from the table, when you are *not* playing, and I agree with them. However, you must think about poker in an ordered way, not as senseless musings. The examples in this book enable you to do this. You can effectively set aside study time and thinking time by reading through the examples you find here.

4. **Give you a detailed analysis of many types of hands.** Many types of hands are described and analyzed, so if you are uncertain as to the best way to play certain hands, or feel that you often play certain hands badly or do not maximize your advantage, you will find specific guidelines here. Not all situations can be covered, of course, but the most common are here.

5. **Give you a detailed analysis of multiple situations.** Poker scenarios are legion, but they still fall into broad theoretical classifications. If you have ever had a situation in which you were unsure as to how to play (and who hasn't?) or wanted to check your play against correct theory and practice, you will likely find here a situation similar to one you faced.

6. **Help you think about poker correctly.** If you read and study the examples, your poker thinking will improve and all aspects of your game will get better. Remember, the essence of poker is making good decisions, but you can only act correctly if you can *think* about poker correctly. The hand examples deepen your understanding of poker theory and enable you to play with more skill and confidence in actual games.

7. **Help you maintain emotional equilibrium during live play.** Losing emotional control, or going on "tilt," is one of the most costly mistakes players make. It is not just about maintaining a

Zen-like demeanor at the table either. Really good players are mostly calm because they understand the theoretical limits of what can happen in poker and have practically seen it all, as it were, through long, and frequently expensive, experience. This has taught them that the only thing you can control is the quality of your decisions. You can steepen your learning curve and reduce any tendency to tilt by absorbing the lessons and "experience" provided within these examples.

8. **Keep up your game even when away from the table.** It is not always possible to play poker. Yes, it's true, sometimes annoying distractions like jobs, families, and social and civic duties mean you cannot play as often as you would like. So when these minor irritations of life impinge upon the serious business of playing poker, how can you prevent yourself from getting rusty and losing your skills? Why, by reading this book, of course! Studying and thinking about these examples is the closest thing to playing when you are *not* playing. Nothing is exactly like a game, but this is close. If you cover the book with a floral paper you can even make others believe that you are reading about gardening and are not absorbed in poker theory!

9. **You can read in any order and focus on any aspect of Hold'em.** You do not have to read this book chapter by chapter, although I recommend that you read the key theoretical concepts first. There are also a number of short but important essays about the no-limit game. Theory is always interlaced with practice. You can, therefore, plug any weaknesses in your game without having to read the whole book.

10. **You will become better, faster.** This is what it is all about. The theory and practice this book offers will enable you to develop as a poker player more quickly and comfortably than in any other way. What you have to do is devote some time to actual study. The alternative could be countless hours of expensive

and frustrating play, where you feel lost and even consider (heaven forfend) giving up poker. So what are you waiting for? Read the book...well...*buy* it first (no reading in the book-shop, please, I can't make money that way), study the examples, and start improving your no-limit Hold'em play!

I'll see you at the table!

How to Use and Get the Most from This Book

Each poker problem in this book covers a specific theme of no-limit Hold'em play. You can jump in at any problem since they are all self-contained or read through them in chronological order. I never give the result of a hand, even if the hand is drawn from a real session. Short-term results don't matter in poker. What matters is making correct decisions. If you keep making correct poker decisions you cannot help but get good long-term results. The outcome of any individual hand is random.

Each problem has a series of choices and I award points for the answer you select. At the end of the book you can total your score and this will give you an idea of where you are as a player. When reading the problems it is important that you examine all the elements of the problem in attempting to arrive at an answer that makes sense and is the most logical given the constraints of that specific problem. Poker, and especially no-limit Hold'em, is a highly situational game; change one or two parameters and the answer to the problem may be radically different, so you must pay attention. No-limit Hold'em is also a game where differing opinions may be held about how to play in any given situation and it is often hard to say which is the best way to play a hand. Stack sizes, your bankroll, your perceived image at the table, your individual style, your playing experience, and the character of the table are all relevant factors in arriving at a correct playing decision and the perception and importance of these create variations of opinion over "the best play." However, the aim of these problems is not to nitpick over fine distinction but to help you avoid the gross errors. These are the ones that cost you money, session after session. No-limit Hold'em is a game in which even experts make mistakes; it is in the very nature of the game. The difference between the expert and the average player is that the experts play in such a way as to ensure that their opponents make more costly mistakes than they do.

When you read this book it is tempting to go immediately to the solution page and just see what I have given as the best answer to any problem that interests you. If you do this you will of course learn things, but you will not really exercise your brain and get the most out of the book. Really try to answer the problems and consider exactly why you believe playing in a certain way is best, *before* looking at the answers. Getting the answer right is less important than learning how to think about the game in a logical way. When you work this way you will progress much more quickly. You may even come to better solutions than mine!

No-Limit Hold'em
Hand by Hand

CHAPTER ONE

Cash Games vs. Tournaments: Key Differences

This book is about the best way to play in fixed buy-in, no-limit Hold 'em cash games, where the buy-ins are between $50 and $1,000. All the problems assume you are playing in a cash game, sometimes called a ring game, and that there is a full table of ten players, unless the problem states otherwise.

Later in this series I will be devoting a whole book to tournament play. Tournament play and cash play have vastly different strategies. It is true that in some of the longer, slower tournaments, like the big buy-in events on the World Poker Tour and at the World Series of Poker, no-limit Hold'em tournaments and no-limit Hold'em cash games share many of the same playing characteristics, especially in the early rounds, but that is where the similarities begin and end.

In tournaments the constantly rising Blinds (and later in the tournament usually Antes) mean that that you frequently have to change pace, alternatively switching between aggressive and cautious play. This creates very different playing considerations from those of a cash game when the Blinds remain constant.

Here are some more differences between tournaments and cash games to consider. Some are obvious, some are not.

- **In tournaments, you have a known downside risk.** Apart from re-buy tournaments, most tournaments have a fixed buy-in. This means that you know from the outset what your downside risk is (at least for that tournament) and therefore that you have an adequate bankroll for that session. Cash no-limit Hold'em by contrast is a dangerous game. Even if you buy in for the minimum, whatever you have on the table can disappear in a single hand. Last night one of my readers (and a student), a good player, lamented how he lost his whole stack: He raised with AQs on the Button and the only caller was the Big Blind. The Flop was A, Q, 7. The Big Blind checked and with top two pair my friend made a pot-sized bet. The Big Blind, who had been playing loose and aggressive poker all evening, re-raised all-in and my friend called with top two pair. Yes, you guessed it, the Big Blind had pocket sevens, flopped a set, and neither player improved on the Turn or River and so my student got stacked. Some pundits may argue that he could have gotten away from the hand but practically speaking, getting stacked like this in no-limit Hold'em is an occurrence that you will experience frequently. My friend lost $600 on one hand. Not a fortune but unpleasant nonetheless. If the same thing had happened in a tournament it would have only cost him the buy-in.

- **Position takes on greater importance in tournaments.** Position is of course important in cash games, but the peculiar nature of tournaments often means that many pots can be won purely by making positional plays. In fact, in a tournament position is often more important than cards. In the next book in the series, which is devoted to tournament no-limit Hold'em, I'll explore this aspect of the game more fully. Right now I just want to tell you that moves made by players in tournaments based solely on positional advantage will simply not work as well when used in a cash game.

- **Stack size means less in cash games.** Stack size is extremely important in tournament play because a player with a big stack can threaten the tournament life of those with small stacks. Come up against the big stack and your tournament may be over fast. No real equivalent exists in cash games. That is not to say that a small stack and a large stack are played the same way in cash games. They are in fact played quite differently. Nor do I mean that having a large stack is not an advantage in cash games, because when you have one plays are available to you that are not available to small stacks. Despite this a player with a big stack in a cash game cannot really use his stack size to bully players in the same way as he can in a tournament. The reasons for this will become clearer as you read this book because I'll describe specific situations, but for now know that you can do very well with a small stack in a cash no-limit Hold'em game against big stacks, if you know what the limitation of small stacks (and indeed big stacks) are and play appropriately.

- **Your earning power must be calculated differently.** Successful tournament players can do very well and earn a high return for money invested. However the ebbs and flows of tournament play are quite different from cash games. A successful cash game player will tend on average to have a winning session about forty to fifty percent of the time. Also, he will usually win more on his winning sessions than he will lose on his losing sessions. Of course dividing poker into "sessions" is artificial but overall winning players will see their bankrolls rise over time even though there may be many valleys and troughs in the upward trend. By contrast even very good tournament players may only cash out infrequently. A successful tournament player playing in multi-table tournaments may have a positive expectation on his play, be in profit, and may still be cashing out less than ten percent of the time. The vast majority of the time the tournament player will simply lose his buy-in. The correct construction of an adequate bankroll for a tournament and a cash player are therefore quite different.

- **You can get a better read on your opponents in cash games.** In a cash game session lasting a few hours, you have plenty of time to observe your opponents and how they play. Observation is important in both cash and tournament poker, but in tournament poker you have far less time to draw a bead on your competition. This is because players are constantly busting out or, as the tournament progresses, you and your opponents are being assigned new seats at different tables and the observation process has to begin from scratch. In cash games, especially if you play against the same people regularly, you can develop a detailed understanding of each person's approach to the game. You can also pick up on any habitual tells they might exhibit. These pieces of information can considerably contribute to your edge in a cash game.

- **Starting hand selections are different.** In tournaments you must frequently modify your starting hand requirements depending on the speed of the tournament, your stack size, and what stage the tournament has reached. Of course, in both cash and tournaments, positional considerations govern starting hand selection, but the fluidity of these considerations is much greater in tournaments than cash games.

- **Bluffing is a bigger weapon in tournament play.** Bluffing has its place in both tournaments and cash games. In cash games, though, there is a lot less bluffing than some players would have you believe. When you play in the smaller cash games, bluffing loses a lot of its value because your opponents are often too unsophisticated to understand what your bluffs mean. This is also the case in the early stages of many tournaments, when many very weak players are still around. These players are hardly ever worth bluffing. However, as the worst players get flushed out, bluffing in tournaments is a key weapon and one that you will almost certainly have to use at some point if you are to stand a chance of finishing in the money. Players who move from tournament play to cash games often bluff too frequently and are surprised when they run into players showing down solid cards at cash tables.

- **You don't have to play short-handed cash games.** If you play in a tournament and you want to finish in the money, you almost always have to play some part of the tournament short-handed. If you get to the final table, and this is often the only place where there is big money, you had better make sure that you can play short-handed poker well. Though many poker tournaments are "chopped" with players at the final table making deals, you often have to play a number of key hands short-handed and you had better know how to do so. In a cash game, by contrast, if the game becomes short-handed, you always have the option to leave, find another game, or take a break and come back if more players fill empty seats. If you don't like or don't play short-handed poker well you can opt not to and it won't affect your profitability.

- **The element of luck is greater in tournaments.** In my opinion this is the biggest downside of tournaments and the biggest benefit of playing cash games. Poker is a game of skill with a considerable element of short-term luck. An ideal poker format balances the elements of luck and skill so that the skillful players win over time but the less skilled and lucky can still occasionally have their day. It ensures that weaker players keep playing and don't just get run over, and that skilled play has its just reward. In fixed buy-in, small stakes no-limit Hold'em played for cash, the skilled player who understands the game, is sufficiently bankrolled, and is disciplined in his play can do very well. This is especially true today as most players still do not play well and there is a constant stream of new and poorly skilled players entering the game. In tournaments, by contrast, due to their structure there is a much greater element of luck. This becomes even greater as the number of players in a tournament increases. The most skilled players still have an edge, but this edge may not practically be realized until they have played scores or even hundreds of tournaments. Thus even the most highly skilled tournament players can have long runs where they do not cash out or only win small prizes. However a skilled cash game player can start out winning almost immediately, and unless they are very unlucky will not have very long runs when they are losing money. For me this is the most attractive aspect of the cash game. This does not mean that you will not experience consecutive losing sessions, getting sucked out on, having poor runs of cards, and getting stacked maybe several times in a session. If you play long enough all of these things will happen to you, but if you play well you will also experience some nice wins along the way where you double, triple, and even quadruple (or more) your stack in a single session.

So there you have it. There are probably some other differences about the two styles of game, but I believe I have covered the major ones. If you think of others that you feel are important, e-mail me at my website www.holdempokernow.com and I'll send you a reply and maybe include them in the next edition. By the way, I believe that tournaments have their place (or I would not be writing a book about how to play them) but I also believe that it behooves players to understand that the two beasts differ and must therefore be fed and nurtured differently.

CHAPTER TWO

Limit Hold'em vs. No-Limit Hold'em: Thirteen Key Differences

When I was playing poker mainly to supplement my income, there were very few no-limit cash games available. Those that existed were usually played for very high stakes that only the richest players could afford. Pot-limit, though the preferred poker style in Europe, was also rarely played in the USA. Limit Hold'em was really the only form of Hold'em in town and was the game of choice for amateurs and professional players alike. The very steady and (relatively) predictable win rates and low fluctuations of the fixed limit game made it an ideal choice for the aspiring professional player. However, due to televised poker and Internet poker sites the popularity of no-limit Hold'em has skyrocketed. If you are making the transition from limit Hold'em to no-limit Hold'em you should read the following points of difference. Failure to understand the very real differences between the games can lead to discomfort at best and disaster at worst.

Do not underestimate the difficulties of transition. I was in Las Vegas not long ago chatting with one of the most knowledgeable and erudite poker authors I know. Those who know him recognize him as a player who has a very complete knowledge of limit Hold'em. In fact he made a decent income from playing middle-limit to high-limit Hold'em in Las Vegas for a number of years. With the growth of no-limit Hold'em he recognized that a lot of the weak money had moved to the no-limit game and so he decided to play no-limit

Hold'em. Now bear in mind that he is a very strong and competent player who has a good understanding of poker theory. He found the no-limit game uncomfortable to say the least. In a few weeks he had lost more than he had in many months playing limit, and although these losses were not outside the realm of statistical possibility for a winning no-limit Hold'em player, he found that they were affecting his play. He, of course, got stacked, sometimes more than once in a session. In his regular limit games he always ensured he had a larger than average stack that he never drained, so he found losing his initial buy-in in no-limit Hold'em disconcerting. He also found that many of the more sophisticated plays he used at limit play were simply ineffective or out of place in no-limit Hold'em. Furthermore, he found the greater psychological element of the no-limit game challenging. After a few months of experimentation with no-limit Hold'em he returned to the limit game where he continues to do very well.

So what can we learn from this? Well, one conclusion that should *not* be drawn is that no-limit Hold'em is a more difficult game than limit Hold'em. Limit Hold'em involves some immensely complex decisions, which would often be made a lot easier if one could bet an unlimited amount in any round. Believe me, limit is complex and has many subtleties and many opportunities for expert play. Players who move from low-limit no-limit Hold'em to middle-range limit Hold'em often feel outclassed and are mostly outplayed. No, I believe that the conclusion we should draw is that the two forms of the game involve different temperaments and this fact should not be taken lightly. Even a knowledgeable player may underestimate this factor. You have to be comfortable in your chosen arena and this is not just a factor of knowledge. The game has to feel right to you if you are to succeed in it. Both forms of the game demand aggression and patience but how these two are applied differ significantly. Also, because my poker expert friend is intelligent and knows himself, he wisely chose to return to the form of Hold'em he not only excelled at but felt emotionally comfortable and competent in. I believe this was a good decision on his part. He has nothing to prove and cleverly plays a form of the game he knows he can usually dominate. Remember, winning and not ego is the name of the game for the professional player.

Below, I have laid out thirteen of the key differences between the two forms of Hold'em. Some are obvious but read them because their implications are not always as obvious. There may be other differences but I think these are the most significant for any player making a transition from one form of the game to another. Even if you are of the younger generation and have never played limit Hold'em, I believe you will benefit from reading these points.

1. **Starting hand selections are more fluid in no-limit Hold'em.** In limit Hold'em it is possible to memorize a chart of starting hands from specific positions and play these with almost no variation. In fact, doing so will plug the biggest weakness in most people's limit game: playing too loosely Pre-Flop. In no-limit Hold'em you must be much more fluid in your starting hand selections especially from late position. Large stacks (and small Blinds) with large implied odds make looser Pre-Flop play correct in no-limit Hold'em because the money in the game is made by skillful Post-Flop play. On the other hand, if you are playing a small stack, starting hand selection from almost any position has to be much tighter than in limit Hold'em because you have *no implied odds*. This fluidity, where your and your opponents' stack sizes affect starting hand selection, can be very confusing and frustrating for players new to no-limit play. It can appear to them that no-limit players have no understanding of card values. If this describes you and you find yourself wondering how some players can do well in no-limit playing "terrible hands Pre-Flop," consider the possibility that there is more that you need to learn about no-limit Hold'em.

2. **You get stacked in no-limit Hold'em.** If you buy in for enough chips to withstand a cap at each round of betting you cannot lose your stack in one hand in limit Hold'em. In no-limit

Hold'em you may lose your whole stack more than once in a session, even if you play flawless poker. You can make an all-in bet with the best hand, get called by a larger stack, and get sucked-out on. It happens a lot. You played correctly but it can be hard to see that stack just go up in smoke. This can cause limit players to tilt or go into a shell and stop playing aggressively enough because they are in constant fear of losing their stack. When playing limit, I always bought in for plenty and therefore even when I had a losing session I never lost my whole stack. Now that I play no-limit Hold'em I have been stacked many times and I have stacked others with both skill and luck. The mental and emotional adjustment you need to make can be challenging, especially if losing your stack happens near the end of a session where you have steadily increased your chips, only to lose them all when an opponent makes a lucky draw. Get used to it. It will never stop happening. You have to look at the long term and realize this event is in the very nature of the game.

3. **You have less play Post-Flop with small and medium stacks in no-limit Hold'em.** If you elect to play with a small stack or are forced by the buy-in rules to play at most a medium-sized stack, many types of plays will not be available to you. A small stack limits your play to Pre-Flop and Flop play, and then mostly to raising with a strong hand and perhaps pushing all-in on the Flop. This can make limit players feel like they cannot use their poker skills to make sophisticated plays on the Flop, Turn, and River. This is true, but that fact changes completely when the stacks are deep in relation to the Blinds. Then play can become very sophisticated.

4. **Individual decisions have greater impact on your winnings and losses.** In limit a bad call or two may lose you a bet or two for a few dollars. Two bad calls in no-limit can cause you to get stacked twice in short order. Bad decisions can be very severely

and quickly punished in no-limit play. The first time I played pot-limit in poker for cash in the UK (also big-bet poker, which is similar to no-limit Hold'em), and somebody bet his stack at me on the Turn I admit I was disconcerted. I had two pair, but the grim prospect of losing my whole stack within minutes of sitting down seemed likely. I called and my opponent had top-pair with the ace kicker and I won, but my heart was beating faster than it ever had when I had made a call in limit poker.

5. **Exactly how your opponents play is more significant in no-limit Hold'em.** A number of limit plays, especially at the lower limits, are almost routine. You can get away with not paying too much attention to exactly how your opponents play. Of course, this is not good limit play but many play like this. In no-limit you must constantly monitor how your opponents play: When they tend to call, raise, or bluff and whether they betray tells are important because you may be making a decision for all your chips. You must watch exactly how they tend to play various types of hands because once you get a good read on someone's playing style then you can start to make plays against them specifically. Since many no-limit pots are heads-up confrontations, knowing how your opponents play becomes very important.

6. **The check-raise is more rarely used in no-limit Hold'em.** The check-raise does have its place in no-limit poker, and sometimes it can be used very effectively. However it is used with far less frequency than in limit play. In limit it is often used because you cannot bet enough to adequately protect a hand, so you check-raise to force opponents to call two bets cold, making an error when they do; or to freeze up bettors so that you can take free cards more often in later rounds of betting. Some limit players are addicted to the check-raise and overuse this valuable tool. In no-limit if you check-raise at all, you must understand precisely how and when to do it most effectively,

because if you use it as you would in many limit situations you may end up trapping yourself, not your opponents. Weapons must be used appropriately and selectively in no-limit and this applies especially to the check-raise.

7. **Draws are often poor value in no-limit Hold'em.** In limit Hold'em and especially in looser games, drawing hands are of great value to players who understand when and how to play them. Pot odds are frequently greater than 4–1 and can even be as high as 20–1 in rare circumstances, making it frequently correct to play drawing hands. In no-limit, where bets can be a third of the pot but on the Flop are more frequently from half the pot size to a full pot size, draws are mostly unplayable. You simply do not have the odds. When draws are played in no-limit without having strictly correct pot odds, it is usually because of implied odds. Many times, however, players overestimate implied odds and use them as an excuse to make weak draws instead of folding. In no-limit you can bet an amount sufficient to protect your hand and take away the odds from drawing hands. You have a big stick to beat your opponents with.

8. **In no-limit, you can and should manipulate the pot by varying bet size.** In limit you have little opportunity to drastically manipulate the pot because, especially in multi-way pots, your bet or even raise achieves little in this regard. In no-limit you can of course bet any amount, so experts bet in such a way so as to manipulate pot size and maximize the errors of less astute players. To do this effectively you must maintain a constant awareness of pot size and how much to bet so as to maximize your advantage. This is in itself a skill that limit players have to learn to develop.

9. **Bluffs and tells are more important in no-limit Hold'em.** In limit Hold'em you bluff at certain times. In no-limit Hold'em, bluffs can be used in many more subtle ways, and if well used,

can greatly increase win rates. To be an effective bluffer, you must be very aware of others' playing patterns and any tells they betray and you must be careful not to betray a tell yourself. You must bluff appropriately in no-limit to be successful and you must learn to spot the difference between the bluffers and those holding the real McCoy. If you fail to learn to bluff or spot the bluffers your play will be either too obvious or you will call too much when you should fold and vice versa. Bluffs and tells take on a higher importance in no-limit Hold'em.

10. **It is often correct to fold to a re-raise or raise in no-limit Hold'em.** In limit Hold'em if you limp before the Flop with, say, four other limpers and the Button raises it is usually correct to call. In fact, folding in these circumstances is usually a gross error in limit play. The reverse is often true in no-limit Hold'em. You may choose to limp with many hands, but it is often completely correct to fold to a raise Pre-Flop. Calling a raise with an inferior hand Pre-Flop will frequently become a costly error.

11. **It is often correct to call on the Button rather than raise in no-limit Hold'em.** In limit Hold'em raising from the Button is usually correct, especially if there are a number of limpers even with a medium-strength hand. In no-limit it is often correct to limp with a wide variety of hands from the Button and see the Flop. With the best position you can make a suitable Post-Flop play. Raising is often a mistake if it only succeeds in opening yourself to a re-raise because you effectively raise yourself out of the pot. Mediocre hands can become very strong hands on the Flop and if you raise at the wrong times when on the Button, you do not give yourself a chance to take advantage of your position on the Flop and beyond.

12. **Position has more importance in no-limit Hold'em.** Hold'em is a highly positional game but no-limit Hold'em is much more

so than limit Hold'em. Positional advantages are so strong in no-limit that you can often win pots without decent cards by using your positional advantage to bet players out of pots or making them afraid to bet. Another consequence of this is that if you play weak cards out of position you are punished much more severely in no-limit than limit Hold'em.

13. **The most skilled players can earn higher win rates with less variance in no-limit Hold'em.** This may be the biggest and most important difference. Expert players in no-limit Hold'em enjoy a far greater comparative advantage over the less skilled than they do in limit Hold'em. In limit, the capacity to only bet and raise specific amounts handicaps the strong and protects the weak. Essentially bad players lose their money more slowly to good players in limit than in no-limit. To some degree this is mitigated by the fixed-limit buy-in in the new low-limit, no-limit games that are on offer. Nonetheless, experts still enjoy a very considerable advantage in no-limit even in this form.

Surprisingly this also means that skilled no-limit players experience less variance and can therefore play with smaller bankrolls at a given level of game than a comparative level at no-limit. No-limit can be deceptive in how big it plays. A $500 fixed buy in a $2–$5 no-limit game is a much bigger game than say a $4–$8 fixed-limit game, even though the players may come to the table with a similar-sized stack. The profit potential in the fixed-limit $4–$8 is probably no more than $8 to $12 per hour (average) even for a very skilled player. It is much harder to ascertain the hourly rate in a no-limit game but a $500 buy in a game can yield $50 to $80 an hour and even more to a skilled player if the opposition is weak. To enjoy this type of return in limit play would require very skilled play against tough opponents at the $40–$80 level, and require a bankroll in excess of $24,000. A skilled no-limit player, playing against mediocre opposition in a $2–$5 Blind game with a buy-in of $500 can succeed with a bankroll of under $10,000.

Of course you only enjoy this advantage if you are a skilled player. If you are moving from limit to no-limit, be careful because you may be joining a much bigger game than you think. This is also the reason why losing players can get through their bankrolls in double quick time in no-limit. Fortunately the maximum buy-ins provide some protection for the less skilled. Before the year 2000 no-limit games were rare, not only because of the lack of TV coverage of poker and the lack of Internet poker, but because the skilled players very quickly blew out the unskilled in no-limit games that had no maximum buy-in. I have seen some casinos that now again offer "small-stakes" no-limit Hold'em *without* a maximum buy-in. It appears that by not learning the lessons of history they are unaware that they are killing the game by making it too unfavorable for the less skilled.

CHAPTER THREE

New No-Limit vs. Old No-Limit: New Skills for a New Poker Age

In the old days (before 2000!), no-limit Hold'em cash games didn't last too long. Every so often a casino, usually in Las Vegas or California, would spread them. Within a short time they stopped attracting all but the very skilled and the very well heeled. Why? Why is it that you can now find some sort of no-limit Hold'em game in almost every casino that spreads poker but even a short time ago they were rarer than Mike Caro's hair combs? Here is why: In no-limit Hold'em the expert has a greater advantage over the non-expert than in any other poker form and this is *especially* true *when the buy-in is unlimited* and *the stacks are deep in relation to the Blinds.* Quite simply the mediocre players were cleaned out PDQ.

To prevent this and to ensure the longevity of poker games, fixed-limit poker arose, where the players' bets and raises were limited. This handicapped the better players somewhat and ensured that players could not lose their whole stack on a single hand, assuming that they had enough chips to at least call the bets and raises through all four betting rounds. Now, this is not a discussion as to whether no-limit Hold'em is harder or easier than limit Hold'em. The fact is that you can lose your whole bankroll super fast in no-limit Hold'em if you don't know what you are doing. In fact, even if you *do* play well, bad beats can be very damaging in no-limit Hold'em and especially when the money is deep. All of the current top cash players, to my knowledge, have been broke at one time or another and this must tell you something about the roller-coaster ride of no-limit Hold'em.

Poker really only began to expand in casinos when fixed-limit poker was introduced and then it began to bloom. To all intents and purposes limit poker was the only commonly available game for most players for years. I believe that without limit poker we would not have had the infrastructure to allow for poker's current boom. By contrast look at poker in the UK (my homeland) and Europe. In both places only pot-limit poker was offered. Even a decade ago in a city as populous as London, only two casinos spread poker. One of those casinos did so only for a short time, and even then only on certain days of the week! The main casino that did spread poker, the Victoria, also had the players self-dealing in the lower limit games, and the facilities were rather pokey, dark, and dingy. Pot-limit poker was restricted to the well versed and well heeled. The lack of limit poker in my opinion is the reason why poker was not more widely played in the UK. *The best players just had too much of an overlay to attract the less skilled.*

Televised poker and Internet poker sites have driven the growth of the game. The average player witnesses the thrill of the big bets and big pots of no-limit Hold'em and wants to give it a whirl. He wants to join in the fun. However, history had shown the casino owners and poker room managers what would happen if deep-stack, unlimited buy-in poker became common: the poker room would lose customers as players busted out and the poker room could die altogether. I do not know where the first game of fixed buy-in no-limit poker was spread but it was a brilliant move. *By limiting the amount of the buy-in, the poker experts were once again somewhat handicapped and whilst weaker players may still lose their whole stack in a hand, it was not so ruinous because they were forced to start with less.*

The buy-in limit has allowed no-limit poker to grow apace across the country and made it possible for a whole new generation of players to enjoy this form of the game. Despite its proliferation many players who have hours of no-limit experience under their belts are still very weak players. How come? Well, when limit poker grew there arose a number of authors such as David Sklansky, Mason Malmuth, Ray Zee, Bob Ciaffone, Jim Brier, Mike Caro, and Lou Krieger (sorry if I omitted any pioneers) who began to write books that gave accurate advice about correctly playing limit poker, especially Hold'em. Seminal works such as Sklansky's *Theory of Poker* and Sklansky and Malmuth's *Hold'em Poker for Advanced Players* became widely available and those who studied and applied their concepts became strong players in a relatively short time. Starting hand values, and themes concerning Flop and Turn play were described at length and new players were attracted to a game that could now be learned without decades of experience involving trial and error. New players could stand on the theoretical shoulders of experts and jump start their poker careers.

Since limit was the dominant form, poker writers tended to restrict themselves to this game. What about the no-limit writers and theorists? To say they were sparse in number is an understatement. Many people have, and still do, describe Doyle Brunson's *Super System* as the "bible of poker." Now whilst that book had a number of insightful essays on different forms of the game from a number of great players and solid writers, I believe the book has become popular and respected for one reason: Brunson, a two-time world champion, offered the only substantial piece of advice on how to play no-limit Hold'em. In fact for years it was the *only* material you could read on no-limit play, apart from snippets and essays in other books. Later on, the great T.J. Cloutier and Tom McEvoy wrote a book and Bob Ciaffone and Stewart Reuben also wrote a volume on big-bet poker that had chapters on no-limit Hold'em, but that was about it.

In recent times other notable writers have penned works on no-limit Hold'em but the only advice players had to go on for years, in book form, were these texts. So is Doyle's approach to no-limit Hold'em still valid? Yes and no. The problem with Doyle's approach and that of some of the older writers is that they are writing about a different game; a game of deep stacks and small Blinds in relation to those stacks. If other players have similarly deep stacks much of their advice remains valid (though perhaps not as detailed as is desirable) but the modern game, especially with current players and smaller stacks, is different. For example much of the bluffing strategy is virtually useless as there is little point in attempting a bluff against a player with a small stack because you will just get called. Hands demanding high implied odds like suited connectors (mentioned as Doyle's favorite in *Super System*) have to be played very selectively because when you play with (or against players with) smaller stacks the high implied odds that make these plays profitable are just not there. So is the answer merely to play tighter? Not exactly. Anyone playing in these games will frequently see five and more callers (seven and eight is not uncommon) before the Flop and a wild range of bets and raises. Sometimes two or more players are all-in by the Turn and side pots involving two or three other players are not uncommon. Also the games described in some of the older books talk about pots of several thousand dollars. For example Doyle Brunson says, on page 600 of *Super System II*:

"If I'm in a game where there is not much money on the table—say, everybody has $5,000 or $6,000..."

and later,

"But it is a totally different story in a big game... if we've both got $250,000 in front of us..."

Most of us are not playing in games where we have a stack of a quarter of a million dollars, so how players at this level think about the game and play it is rather different from you and I if we have a stack of under $1,000 in front of us. I have played at tables where players may have played thousands of Internet no-limit Hold'em games for very low stakes but hardly played any "live-action" poker for more than a few hundred dollars. Players like this and games like this simply did not exist when Doyle wrote *Super System*.

I am not saying that Doyle or any other top player could not beat these types of small stakes, fixed buy-in games if they were so minded. Of course they never venture into them because they are playing in high-stakes games, but if they did, I believe they would be shocked at how the game flows. The $100 or $1,000 buy-in game with Blinds of $1 and $2 or $2 and $5 respectively, and time charges of $10 per hour, probably bears little resemblance to the games the older players have played in, before the current poker boom was under way.

Also TV tournament play is not much of a model for successful play in small- to medium-stakes cash games. Televised poker highlights the spectacular and the bizarre because that is what makes for exciting viewing and TV poker usually features the final hours or even minutes of tournament play when huge Blinds and huge cash differences between players often make for unconventional plays.

This book is about playing no-limit Hold'em under today's playing conditions. It offers practical examples of how to play under specific conditions that you will encounter in casinos all over the world. In short, this book is about *today's* game and the conditions *you* will encounter. The poker world has changed and some very smart people with powerful analytical skills are entering the game. These clever people are developing new insights into the game, and all of us are learning more and more about what constitutes correct play. When and if the advice in this book becomes outdated, I'll revise it, or write a new book. For now you can be confident that this book is relevant to you *now!*

CHAPTER FOUR

A Tale of Two Games: Short Stacks and Deep Stacks

No-limit Hold'em played for cash is really two almost entirely different games: Short stack and deep stack (yes, for the linguistic purists among you it should be "short stack" and "tall stack" or "shallow stack" and "deep stack," but this is the way it is conventionally referred to in poker circles) no-limit Hold'em should be played quite differently. Those of us who have been observing, analyzing, and playing in these newly emerging fixed, buy-in, no-limit games have been aware of this for some time. The first person to talk about it in print was Ed Miller in his book *Getting Started in Hold'em*. In that book he offered a strategy for playing with a short stack in a cash game, and I must say I agree with just about everything he says.

If you work through the poker problems in this volume in chronological order you will observe that the first problems deal with short stack play and the second half of the book with deep stack play. Here is the reason: Short stack no-limit Hold'em is a much more straightforward game than deep stack. Later on I'll explain why, but for now I strongly suggest you familiarize yourself with the principles and examples that show you how to play cash games with a short stack and why you should play this way, especially when you are starting out. If you have played a lot of no-limit Hold'em already, you should still study this section. You will probably learn much and improve your overall game and you may find out some things about short stack play that surprise you. One thing you should know right now is that short stack play in cash games and short stack play in tournaments are utterly different animals. Confusing the two remains one of the fundamental and most costly errors made by players as they begin their cash game careers. In fact I have met a number of players who have been driven away from the cash game because they do not understand this difference. In Chapter One, "Cash Games vs. Tournaments," I described the differences between cash and tournament play but the key point here is that in cash games *large stacks have no inherent advantage over small stacks.* In fact many players would be far better off *only playing short stacks* until their understanding of no-limit Hold'em improves and rests on a much sounder theoretical base.

Why You Should Begin Playing NL Hold'em with a Short Stack

So what exactly is a short stack? The term is multi-faceted: In a fixed buy-in game it is often the minimum amount you can buy in for, frequently 20 percent of the stated maximum. This percentage varies widely from card room to card room, however. In some you have to buy in for more, 30 percent or 50 percent of the maximum, and in some the minimum and maximum are the same; in other words in a $500 fixed buy-in game, you *have* to buy in for $500, no more and no less. Even in these games this may well mean you have the shortest stack at the table, if the game has been going on for a number of hours and other players have busted out or left. Some may have stacks many times more than the maximum buy-in and some may be nursing a very short stack. It is not uncommon to begin a game and have every other player's stack cover yours (they have more chips). If you have less than 25 times the Big Blind, you can call this a short stack.

Players who come from the world of tournament no-limit Hold'em are worried about entering a game in which every other player has them covered because they believe that this offers an inherent advantage to the big stacks. It feels like they are beginning with a handicap. In tournament play this is quite correct, but in cash play this is entirely irrelevant if you understand how to play with a short stack. Here is why: In a tournament you may gather many chips over the hours you play but these mean nothing if you do not at least finish in the money. In fact, to make the tournament profitable (unless it is a very large one, like the World Series of Poker Main Event) you usually have to at least make the final table. The fundamental requirement is that you must survive and also gather chips, to use as a weapon. *How* you survive, gather chips, and prosper is the subject of another book, but survive you must. This means that players with big stacks can effectively bully the small stacks by mere aggression because the small stack player's tournament life is on the line every time he is up against the big stack. The big stack becomes a powerful weapon. Unless you are in a re-buy tournament you cannot play on if you are busted out so you have to be cautious when playing against the big stack.

By contrast, in a cash game you can simply buy in again if you're busted out. The only money you risk is, of course, the money you put on the table. If you raise with AA Pre-Flop, for example, in a $2–$5 $500-maximum buy-in game, and are then re-raised, you will probably go all-in with, say, a $100 short stack. If you get called by a player who has a $3,000 stack, what does it matter? You have begun as a clear favorite and have gotten all your money in when you have the best hand. If you win $100 from your deep-stacked opponent, it still buys you a coffee and a sandwich in Manhattan and the most your deep-stacked friend can win from you if you take a bad beat is $100. Some players maintain that playing with a small stack means you are more likely to get called, you cannot use your big bet as a weapon to push another player off a hand, and you cannot really bluff. This is true, but to that complaint I respond, "So what?!" When playing a small stack, *you* cannot be bluffed and players are forced to play a much smaller range of hands against you *because your small stack does not offer your opponents the necessary implied odds to play the types of hands that only profit from high implied odds and, therefore, deep stacks.*

This means that the correct strategy for small stack no-limit Hold'em is to play very tightly Pre-Flop and to try to get your whole stack in Pre-Flop or on the Flop. By playing tight you will usually be starting with the better hand and your opponents can do nothing on the Turn and River except watch the cards. You'll enjoy the fact that as a short stack you will get called more often because you will usually be called by inferior hands. You will get your money in the middle when you have the best of it. The very essence of winning money in no-limit Hold'em is to get players to call you, or make large bets with inferior hands to yours and ensure that they make as little as possible with their winning hands. Short stacks fit the bill nicely because they achieve both ends. Short stacks played this way also ensure that you cannot make any mistakes on the Turn and River because once you are all-in, there are no poker decisions left to make. You effectively reduce Hold'em to a two-betting-round game.

One other important point to emphasize is that the *inherent advantages of playing a small stack only apply when your opponents have much deeper stacks than you.* This is especially true if your opponents have very large stacks and are willing to play more loosely against each other, which as you will discover later in the book is a perfectly legitimate strategy when deep stacks play against each other. When you enter a hand playing very tight, you will often have a significant advantage over your opponents. They, however, may be less concerned about you and instead play against each other, creating a side pot on the Turn and River that may easily exceed the main pot. You may win the main pot and have no equity in the (bigger) side pot, but again, who cares? You can easily double and triple your stack in double-quick time in a game like this, and whilst this may prove irritating to your big-stacked opponents, there is nothing they can do about it. Unlike in a tournament, there is no point in the bigger stacks checking down a hand to gang up on you to knock you out, because knocking you out is not a possibility. Winning money from your opponents is!

I am not arguing that playing no-limit Hold'em short stacked is the most profitable way to play, but it is by far the simplest way to play and beat most no-limit Hold'em games. It is a terrific starting point if you are new to no-limit Hold'em, have just entered a game with players you are unfamiliar with, are moving up in game size and are not quite comfortable at the new limit, or if you wish to give yourself the highest chance of protecting your bankroll. In his book *Ace on the River*, ultra high-stakes player Barry Greenstein comments that he usually buys in for the minimum. If this is how one of the world's best cash no-limit Hold'em players behaves, then perhaps it makes sense for you too!

Deep Stack Play

Playing no-limit Hold'em with a deep stack is a much more complex game. It requires a far greater range of skills and a deeper understanding of no-limit poker than playing with a short stack. Played well against weak opposition (and weak is a relative term), it may well offer the highest profit potential of any poker form. Of course, if you are outclassed or are having a very bad run of cards, it can put a mighty hurtin' on your bankroll too. To play no-limit Hold'em as an expert, you are going to have to study and practice the deep stack game eventually. The reason for this is that if you want to win the most money possible from your poor-playing, deep-stacked opponents, you ideally want to have at least as much as they do in their stacks. In this way you smite them with mighty force when they make those big mistakes on the Flop, but especially when they play badly on the Turn and River. This is where the gap between the expert and the duffer is at its most pronounced. Weak, deep-stacked players can lose their money so fast that a no-limit poker game can disappear from a card room. After all, the casino makes its money by time charges and rakes so it wants the games to last a long time and attract and keep new players, at least for a while. This brings us full circle as to why these types of big (or un-limited) stack, small Blind games are less evident and why they are probably bad for the game as a whole (but good for the experts that play in them!) and tend to become less popular over time. If you start short stacked and pile up some chips, then by Jove, you may find yourself playing a medium or even large stack in relation to your opponents. Now your skill at deep stack play will bear fruit.

It is for these reasons that the majority of the problems in this volume deal with elements of deep stack play. Study them and learn the principles involved, and your no-limit Hold'em game can only improve.

CHAPTER FIVE

Starting Hands and Playing Styles in No-Limit Hold'em

G ood Hold'em play is built upon a solid foundation of correct starting hand play. It is certainly true that the easiest way to make a major improvement in your game is by memorizing a set of starting hands in early, middle, and late position and sticking to them rigorously. At least this is true for limit Hold'em. One of the biggest weaknesses of bad players is poor starting hand selection. Historically it has been easy to improve this part of the game, however, because many authors, most notably David Sklansky and Mason Malmuth, laid out a table that described which starting hands to play from various positions and given particular game conditions. These starting hand recommendations have been debated across various books and poker forums both in print and over the Internet. Some authors have questioned some of the rankings and cogent arguments have been advanced for favoring some hands over others, but at least such charts and tables give players new to Hold'em a place to start.

Taking these same ideas, concepts, and starting hand selections to no-limit Hold'em is not as easy as it at first appears. Many limit players have merely transferred their concepts of "correct" Pre-Flop play from the limit to the NL Hold'em and seem bemused and occasionally angry that they often don't translate. To their dismay and consternation they have seen their whole stack disappear to a player who "must be crazy to call a raise from that position with those two cards."

Now sometimes this is indeed just poor play being rewarded by luck as is frequently the case in poker, but many players used to limit Hold'em starting hand values fail to recognize that when playing no-limit Hold'em they aren't in Kansas anymore. Many factors determine when and how a specific hand is playable Pre-Flop in NL Hold'em. Sklansky and Malmuth's poker starting hands arose as a result of a deep understanding and analysis of the limit game. Players who are just copying these ideas by rote have not learned how to modify these starting selections where necessary to NL Hold'em.

Starting hand selection is a much more fluid thing in NL Hold'em than in limit Hold'em. This is especially true in the deep-stack game because the high implied odds mean that hands can rapidly change value on the Flop and beyond. For example, say a player enters the pot with AA but comes in for a small raise, because he wants action. He is effectively slowplaying Pre-Flop. However, whilst he clearly starts with the best hand, a poker hand is made of five cards, not two. His slowplay may allow a player with, say, 7,6s to enter the pot quite cheaply and "see a flop." Now if the Flop comes J, 7, 6 the player with AA may lose a lot of money if he does not know how to play well on and beyond the Flop. His hand has, unknown to him, become a big underdog. In limit Hold'em this may cost him a bet or two. In NL Hold'em it can cost him his whole stack or a substantial part of it if he does not know how to play. *When the player called the raise with 7,6s he was not aiming at the pot plus a few bets, he was aiming at the raiser's whole stack. Remember, in NL Hold'em you make the most money when you induce players with weaker hands than yours to call or make large bets.*

It is this consideration that greatly affects starting hand selection in NL Hold'em. Alongside this is the question of *your* stack size, which I will discuss a little later because stack size greatly alters hand selection. If you have a deep stack and you are playing against deep stacks, you must also consider your individual playing style.

The Spectrum of Playing Styles

In his excellent book *Harrington on Hold'em* (which is about tournament NL Hold'em), Dan Harrington identified three different playing styles that he labeled conservative, aggressive, and super-aggressive. The conservative player has a fairly limited range of starting hands that he is willing to play from specific positions. Like limit Hold'em, this range of hands increases as he moves into later positions if there has been no Pre-Flop raising. Aggressive and super-aggressive players play a much wider variety of hands and in the case of super-aggressive players, starting hand values are barely a consideration. Perhaps the most famous and successful of the aggressive tournament players of the past was Stu Ungar, who remains the only player to have won the World Series of Poker three times. His intelligent and fearless playing style made him a feared opponent.

The aggressive and super-aggressive styles have serious drawbacks, though. The primary one is that because a player adopting this style mostly begins each hand with less-than-premium values, the play on the Flop and beyond usually demands much greater skill, because the aggressive players will frequently find themselves having to make more complex poker decisions. It is very tempting to adopt this swashbuckling playing style that involves aggression, a lot of bluffing, a lot of action, and constantly putting your opponents under pressure by betting and raising pot after pot. Again, televised poker has added to the apparent attractiveness of this style as many of the top players one sees on television seem to play this way. For some players it is the only way to play "macho poker" (even if you are a woman!), and anything else is scorned as timid, weak, and rock-like. Until, that is, you have burned through a few bankrolls playing this way. It is hard to find a top-ranked aggressive or super-aggressive player who has not completely blown their entire bankroll at least once and many have done this several times. The subsequent war stories about scraping together another bankroll, borrowing money from poker buddies or Great-aunt Mabel, playing smaller stakes, and gradually building their bankroll so that they can play "the big game" certainly have romantic appeal and make for exciting TV and magazine interviews, but living like this has little appeal to me. I believe that when playing cash games and especially if you are a no-limit Hold'em novice, you are far better off adopting a conservative playing style. Still not convinced? Here are what I see as the major problems with the aggressive and super-aggressive styles:

1. **You are not as good as you think.** Self-effacing humility is rarely a problem I observe in poker players. Unlike golf, tennis, or even chess, in poker the large element of luck makes it difficult to see when you are completely out-classed. Consequently, many players delude themselves for years, believing that they are much better than they are and putting their losses down to bad luck. This seems to be a phenomenon at all levels. It is a rare player who knows himself and his limitations. As I have stated above, the aggressive style demands high levels of skill to be effective and quite simply most players cannot bring it off. Of course, the big wins this playing style can bring, even if wielded by the inept, continues to foster the deluded belief in bad players that they can continue to play this way and succeed as long as they get their fair share of cards. Funny how that fair share never seems to materialize though.

2. **The style is more suited to tournament than cash play.** In the chapter Cash Games vs. Tournament I have highlighted some of the major differences between the two games and I won't repeat them here, but it is worth noting that aggressive styles most often succeed in tournament play. Aggressive players often have trouble adjusting to the different demands of no-limit Hold'em played for cash. Running over a table is much harder to do in a cash game where players are not threatened by elimination and a stack shrinking in relation to rapidly increasing Blinds.

3. **In smaller stakes games outright aggression is less effective.**
   If three or more players are seeing the Flop, you'd better have
   decent cards. It is relatively easy to move one player off a hand
   with aggressive play. Two players can be browbeaten, but if the
   pot is contested by three or more players there is a good chance
   that one player is going to play back at you or at least look you
   up. You usually need top pair or better to win a pot that is contested by three or more players, because there is a good chance
   you will have to showdown the winning hand to take the pot.
   The aggressive style loses a lot of ground when pots are contested by multiple opponents. Three or more players seeing the
   Flop is common in NL games where the maximum buy-in is
   $1,000 or less. If the buy-in is $100 maximum, almost every pot
   is multi-handed and you often have to showdown the best
   hand to win.

4. **You end up trapping yourself.** Your clever trapping and aggressive play will mean little to less sophisticated opponents
   and when they play solid cards against you they will often
   have to do little more than check or call (passive players want
   to play like this anyway) to beat you when you are running a
   bluff or over-betting poor hands. You will trap yourself as
   often as you trap others, by using plays that are too fancy for
   the smaller games.

   5. **It's tiring to play the aggressive styles.** Playing the aggressive style demands great skill when playing on the Flop and
   beyond, as you will be faced with many more complex poker
   decisions than a conservative player will face. If you are not
   playing at the top of your game, your decision quality can de-
   cline fast and your results along with it.

6. **You need a larger bankroll.** The aggressive styles are often a
   roller-coaster ride. You can blow a number of stacks making
   brash moves and you can take down some huge pots when

you catch cards and nobody gives you credit for holding any decent hands. You give a lot of action and you get lots too. Your bankroll can suffer some serious downswings playing this way. It is easy to believe that downswings will not affect you emotionally or psychologically when they come, but don't you believe it. When you have lost 70 percent of your bankroll, it is not easy to make great poker decisions. Also the swashbuckling style usually demands that you buy in for a large sum so that you can use a large stack to intimidate your opponents with the prospect of being stacked when they play against you.

So my recommendation is to play in a conservative manner until your skills improve and not be timid but selectively aggressive. You will build a solid game that will make you hard to beat in cash NL Hold'em.

Specific Starting Hand Recommendations

I am now going to talk about how to play specific hands Pre-Flop. None of my recommendations are set in stone and since poker is a situation-dependent game, there may be times when you vary from these suggestions. If you stick to them and understand the reasoning behind my suggestions, however, you will have the basis of a very solid, but rather conservative Pre-Flop strategy. These recommendations are based upon the idea that you have a medium to large stack in relation to the Blinds. You must always ask yourself the question:

WHEN I PLAY THIS STARTING HAND, WHAT HAND AM I BUILDING?

In other words what Flops will you like and which ones will make playing hard? Also, as the stacks get deeper the value of a hand Pre-Flop derives from its capacity to win money from your opponents on the Flop and beyond, and because of this a strict ranking based upon how they win in a showdown (or any other strict ranking for that matter) is of no value.

In early position you must be extremely selective when playing starting hands in NL Hold'em. From late position it is almost impossible to make specific recommendations because the effects of position and your stack size in relation to your opponents' stack sizes open up so many possibilities.

At the end of this section I will give a set of starting hands for selections for playing a short stack. Short stack cash play is relatively straightforward but demands very strict and tight starting hand selections to be successful, because of the relative absence of implied odds. When playing a short-stack you will usually be all-in on the Flop, when you mostly have a clear advantage and the best hand. Effectively you will reduce the game to almost two betting rounds. If you do not play the Turn and River, you cannot make mistakes on them. You also cannot make bluffing plays or any sophisticated Turn and River plays. Guess what? When you play this way then your opponents cannot make them against you either. When you have a short stack, you force them to play short-stack poker too. If they don't know how to play it properly, you gain an enormous advantage. Short stack is usually the way for new players to go, until they learn the subtleties of no-limit Hold'em.

AA

You would think that the strongest starting hand in Hold'em is fairly easy to play, and it is if you have reasonable expectations. An unreasonable expectation is that pocket aces will always win. It is also just as unreasonable to say, "I can never win with aces." I have even heard some players say they hate aces. Idiots. You have the best starting hand and you should raise and re-raise with it from any position. Of course, you would love to be all-in with aces before the Flop, but this is rarely possible. Slowplaying aces Pre-Flop is a theoretical mistake and usually a practical one too. In very tight games you may pick up aces in early position, raise, and find that everyone folds. It is disappointing to only pick up the Blinds but you should still raise. You are of course hoping that one of your opponents has picked up a hand he likes and is willing to call or reraise. Aces are always a favorite but you want to commit your chips early in the hand. Aces play well in multi-handed pots and of course heads up. However, the mathematics of the situation indicate that you are quite happy to reduce the field, especially if you can get your money in Pre-Flop. Against one opponent holding random cards, aces will win 85.4 percent of the time if both players go to the showdown. Against six opponents, though, this drops to 43.5 percent. However in the smaller NL games, it is not uncommon for four people to see the Flop. If three have decent hands such as a KK, JJ, or even T9 suited and one has a poor hand, say 8,7 off-suit, your winning percentage with aces drops to about 43 percent.

I recommend that you raise at least three times the Big Blind with aces and raising four to five times is fine. In some $1–$2 Blind games an opening raise of $8–$12 is often standard. If it is raised to you by this amount re-raise to at least $25 or even $40, and you are likely to still get action. If you are opening for a raise in this type of game do not be afraid to raise to $20 with aces.

Some experts have recommended calling with aces or putting in a small raise, in early position. The idea is that if it is raised behind you, you can re-raise for a substantial amount when the action gets back to you. This is an interesting way to vary your play of aces, but it only works if you know players behind you are aggressive. A call or minimum raise in a small-stakes, fixed buy-in NL game is likely to attract lots of callers, any of whom may Flop a hand like two-pair or a set and give you a hard Post-Flop decision with your pair of aces.

KK

You have the second best hand in Hold'em. In most circumstances you will play this hand just like AA. Of course the *only* hand you really fear is AA, before the Flop. A story: About two years ago

I was playing in a small stakes game at the poker room of The Hotel at Mandalay Bay in Las Vegas. A solid player was on my right in early position and on my left was the largest stack at the table, who was also a fair player. The solid player to my left put in a small raise; I folded, having no hand; and the big stack raised about twice the pot. Everyone folded and when the action got back to him, the solid player pushed all-in. Even though the big stack had him covered, losing a pot of this size would have put a major dent in his stack. The minute I saw the solid player move all-in, I left the table and whispered to my wife, who was just outside the poker room, "Aces." The big stack thought for about two minutes and then called the all-in bet. The solid player did indeed have the aces and the big stack, pocket kings. The solid player had made a small raise, hoping a player behind would re-raise so that he could move all-in. The scenario was perfect for him, as the kings held by a player with a big stack are the most likely to give him exactly this action. So having made this masterful read would I have folded the kings? *No!* Frankly, I know of no good player who would, and I doubt anybody who claims they would. It is easily possible that our solid player held QQ (KK are less likely as two kings are accounted for), JJ, or AK and if so the kings are way ahead. You can at best put opponents on a *range* of hands not a specific hand, especially Pre-Flop, so in my opinion the call was correct, just unlucky.

If you play pocket kings and an ace Flops you have to size up your opponents. In a multi-way pot (if your Pre-Flop raise has not thinned the field, and you did raise, didn't you?) you may perhaps bet one third to half the pot if it is checked to you, but if you get any resistance it is likely that one of your opponents holds an ace. Heads up you should probably also make a similar bet, representing an ace. A player holding an ace with a weak kicker or say QQ, JJ, or TT will be hard pressed to continue. You are going to be betting on the Flop most times if you are not all-in Pre-Flop. An exception might be if the Flop was single suited and neither king was of that suit.

If you hold KK and it is raised, re-raise from any position. Move all-in if you face a raise and re-raise.

QQ, JJ

These are hands that you really prefer to either play heads up or in a multi-handed pot when you make money by flopping a set. If you are going to play for the set, then these hands play the same as a small pair, but of course they have value in themselves as they can win unimproved. Some players prefer to only call with these hands and then look at the Flop, hoping not to find overcards. This is *not* the best way to play them. Instead you should raise with these hands at least 80 percent of the time from any position in an un-raised pot. If there have been a number of callers and you are in late position, then you must put in a raise large enough to get some of the limpers to fold. Ideally you want to have only one or two opponents seeing the Flop with you. Exactly how much you should raise is a function of the game you are in. If you are first in, raise four to six times the Big Blind, from any position. If you are in middle or late position and a player in front of you raised three times the Big Blind, for example, re-raise to try and get heads up, as only AA, and KK (QQ too if you hold JJ) are beating you.

What if you face a re-raise? If you face a raise and re-raise Pre-Flop fold these hands. You are probably in a marginal situation. Wait for better opportunities.

TT–99

Some experts view TT as a premium hand. If you can play it heads up from late position against passive players then raise three to five times the Blind, especially if there are no limpers. Other than that I believe that like 88–22, these pairs should be played for a set. In small-stakes games many players will play with suited aces and kings and if an ace or king flops, they will not give them up easily. I believe these hands have little value unless they flop sets. Don't get married to them if all you have is a pair, or an overpair on the Flop and the action is hot and heavy.

What if you face a raise? Fold these hands to a raise from early position. You can call a standard raise from middle position but only continue if the Flop hits you big.

88–22

With these hands you usually have to hit a set to win. Most Flops will contain at least one overcard. Sets are the classic hand that often allows you to double through an opponent. Their value lies in the fact that your hand is so well disguised. If one of your opponents is unwilling to release top-pair, or makes two-pair, or is willing to stand a lot of heat if they choose to play a draw, sets become even more profitable. It is for these reasons that a pocket pair has even greater value in no-limit play than in limit play. The implied odds if you hit your set are enormous. The odds of making a set on the Flop are 1:7.5 against. However, you don't need to have seven or eight Pre-Flop callers to make calling correct, again because of disguise and implied odds. Conversely it is almost impossible to laydown a set. Even a single suited Board may make a set impossible to get away from.

The nice thing about small pairs is that if you don't make a set on the Flop, it is very easy to get away from them. *In an unraised pot these pairs are all playable from middle position forward. In the Blinds you would also play them in an unraised pot.*

In early position a lot depends on the type of game you find yourself in. If the players are passive you can probably play them in early position. If the players behind you are aggressive and liable to raise and re-raise you are probably better off folding these in early position because if you call and the raises are large you really should release the hand and not see the Flop. The exception to this would be if you and your opponents were very deeply stacked and the raises were small in relation to your stacks. Then you may call such raises but again this is back to implied odds. You are taking aim at your opponent's whole stack, not just calling on the basis of pot odds. Calling in such circumstances will also increase your bankroll fluctuations considerably.

In middle or late position I would call a raise if that raise were not larger than five times the Big Blind, and players behind were usually passive. Again, if I did not Flop a set I am usually gone. If I

Flop an overpair to the Board I would bet, but fold in the face of a re-raise.

Pocket pairs have great potential in no-limit Hold'em and you usually want to see the Flop when you have them. If you are raised Pre-Flop and you will be facing only one or two opponents on the Flop, then you're usually better off folding these hands. In my experience too many players use the concept of implied odds as an excuse for loose calling in no-limit Hold'em. Pairs are valuable but you still want to see a multi-handed pot to play the smaller ones. Fold these hands to a raise from early position.

AKs, AK

Sometimes AKs and AK can get players into hot water. I think this is because players forget what they are building. With both hands you are looking to flop top pair. If you flop trip kings or aces, you are unlikely to get a lot of action, and if you flop a draw it is usually to an inside straight. AKs is a very powerful hand, if you flop a flush or a flush draw, but if not, you just have two big cards. Any pair beats you.

The danger is getting married to the hand after the Flop if you flop only overcards or top pair. Realize that top pair is a hand that you usually only want to contest a small pot with. If players are betting and raising on the Flop or beyond when you have top pair then in the smaller stakes games this usually means that you are beaten.

What if you face a raise? Re-raise in an attempt to get heads up with the raiser. AK does not play well in multi-way pots.

AQs, AQ

AQs and AQ are very difficult hands to play in NL Hold'em, because your hand is easily dominated. It is hard to get away from them when you have flopped an ace, but so costly when you are against an aggressive opponent with AK. I suggest that you play AQs primarily as a drawing hand. You can raise with it from early, middle, or late position but beware if you have multiple callers. If you don't flop a flush, straight, or draw, you must play the hand carefully. Do not become over-committed to top-pair.

AQs is a great hand to fold to an early position raise in no-limit Hold'em. If I hold the hand in late position and someone comes in for a standard raise in, say, middle position I may call if I know the raiser to be loose Pre-Flop. Even then I am playing it for its flush potential. If an ace flops and there are bets and raises when the action gets to me I usually pass. Doyle Brunson says he never plays AQ. If you did likewise I don't believe you would be giving up much and you will probably save yourself hard decisions in marginal situations.

AJs–A9s, KQs

These are hands that can trap you easily and cost you many pots because it is hard to know where you are when you make top-pair. I prefer to fold these hands unless I am in late position and I then call if there are limpers or raise if first in. With limpers I am aiming for a flush and with one or two opponents I am usually playing for a small pot that I hope to win on the Flop. Unless you flop a flush or straight these are not hands to play in a big pot in no-limit Hold'em. About the only place I will play AJ unsuited is on the Button if I am first in, and then for a raise. I will make a continuation bet on the Flop if it is checked to me, but if I encounter any resistance on a threatening Flop, I am out.

The real value of these is for their flush potential and you should really be looking to release them on the Flop unless you have made a big hand or have a strong draw.

OTHER SUITED CONNECTORS

When the stacks are deep suited connectors can win a big pot. This is because they are often well disguised on the Flop and if they make a flush, straight, or two small pair they can win a nice pot. This assumes that you have an opponent who is willing to play aggressively or continue to call on the Turn and River with top-pair, when you have, say, two-pair. They can also be very good hands against players who habitually slowplay AA or KK Pre-Flop and then overplay the same hands when they have an overpair to the Flop. If you make a flush, straight, or two pair, you may be able to stack them. However, these hands work when they work because of high implied odds. You may be able to call a raise with these if you are in middle- to late-position, believe that you are unlikely to be re-raised, and calling represents between about 5 to 10 percent of your stack. If you are re-raised behind, you should fold. Remember, the above playing conditions have to be present, otherwise you can only play these hands profitably from late position when you call a number of limpers.

NON-SUITED CONNECTORS: KQ, KT, QJ, JT, QT, T9

Again if you know what you are building these hands can be played in late position and sometimes in middle position in an un-raised pot. Personally unless I am on the Button looking to flop a straight or straight draw I will not play with these hands. The chances of being dominated are just too great. If for example you call an early position raise with these hands and you flop top-pair it makes it very hard to know how to play on. So unless you flop a made hand, a draw, or possibly trips or two pair you really do not want to play big pots with these hands. These are the trap hands of Hold'em. If you never play them you will probably still do very well.

SUITED CARDS

Suited cards are like the siren song for some no-limit Hold'em players who have to play them living in hope of the goddess-like flush. However, being suited is not in itself enough to make a hand worth playing, so unless that hand is one of the hands already mentioned *and suited*, fold it.

GAPPED CARDS

If not already mentioned, these are rarely worth playing unless you are on the Button and no players have raised, or in the Small

Blind for half a bet. It is easy to throw a lot of money away playing these from early and middle position, as you will have to throw them away to most raises and create potentially difficult playing decisions on the Flop and beyond. You don't need to play a lot of hands to do well in cash no-limit Hold'em.

Any hand I have not specifically mentioned should be folded Pre-Flop. Please read the next section on Button play for special exceptions.

Special Considerations for Play on the Button

Position is such a powerful factor in NL Hold'em that it is almost impossible to give specific starting hand recommendations, especially when the stacks are deep and the Blinds low in relation to those stacks. Essentially you must play well on the Flop and beyond to take maximum advantage from your position on the Button. You also have to observe the other players carefully. What you play and how you play the hand, may change radically in late position depending on what you determine about your opponents' playing styles and what image you have at any given table. The problems in this book reflect these considerations.

In an unraised pot with more than three limpers many, many hands become playable from the Button, but you must recognize how you stand on the Flop and the meaning of your opponents' checks, bets, and raises. You cannot play a mechanical strategy. This is not to say that loose calling of bets and raises is good Pre-Flop Button play or good Post-Flop Button play. The Button gives you a chance to assess and analyze the information that is being revealed by your opponents' play, but you must use your powers of observation and analysis to take advantage of that information. Plays on the Button have the potential power to make you a lot of money, but you have to use that power wisely, not recklessly.

Starting Hands for Small Stack Play

If you have a small stack in relation to your opponents' or if your opponents have much smaller stacks than yours, no limit Hold'em is in fact a much easier game than most people imagine when played like this. Essentially, the game is reduced to one of two betting rounds where you are getting all your chips in on Pre-Flop or on the Flop if you have the small stack. The more sophisticated plays are not available to you but you can play a winning game by playing tight Pre-Flop. How tight? Ultra-tight. You will still get action because there are many loose and unobservant players who will call your raises with inferior hands. I often play this way and buy in for the minimum until I develop an understanding of the players and the game I find myself sitting in.

Here are the starting hand requirements I recommend. They will probably seem unbelievably tight but you must play this way with a small stack in a cash game. Loose play with small stacks will just result in losing buy-in after buy-in. These are your starting hand requirements by position:

Early Position: AA, KK, QQ, JJ, AK (suited), AK. Yes, I don't even consider TT worth playing up front.

Middle Position: Same as early position plus TT, AQ (suited). Again I don't bother with AQ or AJ or KQ.

Late Position: Same as early and late but you can add 99, 88, 77, AQ, AJ (suited and non-suited), AT (suited), KQ (suited and non suited).

When entering the pot with these hands open for as large a raise as you believe your opponents will call. On the Flop you should usually just push all-in, unless perhaps the Board is single suited and you have no cards of that suit or the action indicates you may be trailing.

If you have three or more Pre-Flop limpers and you are on the Button you can call with any pocket pair and any suited ace. Of course now you will have to play the Flop. Continue if you make a set or if you make a flush. If you make two pair with your suited ace, you are probably leading and can make a pot-sized bet on the Flop. If you Flop a flush draw, bet if you believe that doing so will win you the pot immediately.

DEALING WITH RAISES

If there is a raise in front of you that is a standard raise of three to five times the Big Blind or whatever the standard is for your game, re-raise with AA, KK, QQ, JJ, and AK (suited or not) and fold everything else. If there is a raise and a re-raise, move all-in with AA and KK and fold the rest.

If you or your opponent's remaining stack is less than twice the size of the original bet you can move all-in with any of your raising hands.

PLAYING AGAINST LIMPERS

Your aim is naturally to get your money in when you have the greatest advantage, usually Pre-Flop. The easiest way to do this is to bet all-in Pre-Flop, but of course this will rarely be effective. Very strong hands will call and weak hands will fold. Your objective is to get weaker hands than yours to play a pot against you when you have the best of it so you must size your bet accordingly. If you play the above hands you must put in the *largest raise Pre-Flop that your opponents are likely to call.* You must watch the game carefully to see what amount this is. It may be three to five times the Big Blind but in small-stakes games it is often a lot more. Of course you must vary the size of your raise, because your opponents will believe you are playing a much greater range of hands than you in fact are and you must foster this belief so that they call with weaker hands.

If you get called and see a Flop you should move all-in if it is checked to you and your stack is less than or approximately the size of the pot.

Your hardest decisions will be when you check your option in the Big Blind. You then have to judge whether you have the best hand on the Flop in an unraised pot. If you believe you do, and your stack is much larger than the pot, bet an amount approximately two-thirds to a full pot size. Do the same if the action is checked to you, whatever you hold. If your opponents play back at you, you must either fold or move all-in. Make your best judgment and do what you think best. Even if you are wrong, you are only making a mistake for a small sum. On the Turn, if you have any chips left, check and fold if you feel you do not have the best hand, but if you think your hand is leading or has just a 50 percent chance of winning push all-in.

Remember the overall short-stack strategy: Get as much money in as early as you can when you almost certainly have the best hand. This means you usually want to be all-in on the Flop or if at all possible before. This way you bet with the best of it and eliminate errors on the Turn and River because you have nothing left to bet.

I repeat, everything above is a guide. I hope you find it useful.

CHAPTER SIX

The Problems

Problem One: Cowboys

Theme: Small Stack Play Pre-Flop Big Pair

Stack Size: Small

Position: Middle

You have just bought into a $2–$5 game for the minimum buy-in of $100; the maximum being $500. This will be the game size and buy-in for all the problems that involve playing a small stack. Also (though it never happens), it is assumed that there is no rake or time charge, for ease of calculation. You decided to post $5 and not wait for the Big Blind because you wanted to get into action immediately. You are in middle position. Every other player at the table has you covered, that is, has a stack size greater than yours.

Player B, in early position, has called for $5. The other players have folded and the action is on you. You look down and are pleasantly surprised to find the cards pictured on the next page:

Do you:

- · Raise all-in for your remaining stack of $95?
- · Raise three to five times the Big Blind?
- Call?
- Fold?

If you answered "fold"...please close the book and hit your head repeatedly against a wall until you feel better! Obviously you are going to play the hand, but how? With a pair of kings in this situation you want, if possible, to get all your chips into the pot before the Flop because you are just about certain to have the best hand right now with only a pair of aces beating you. No player has shown strength yet, but other players may raise behind you.

If you answered "call," give yourself one point. Of course it is not as bad as folding but you may find that many players call behind you and this is not the best scenario for pocket kings. Ideally you want to be up against one player who has called or raised *you* with an inferior hand and you contest the pot heads up.

Some players call here hoping to re-raise all-in if another player raises. This slowplay Pre-Flop is often a losing play (unless you have very aggressive players behind you who are raising very frequently) because either you get no raise and give many players a chance to out-flop you, or when you re-raise all-in the original raiser smells a rat and just folds, winning you merely a small pot for your Pre-Flop monster.

If you answered "raise all-in," give yourself two points. This is not the worst play but is unlikely to get you a call. It screams, I have a big pocket pair! All but the loosest players will fold and you will pick up the Blinds plus the $5 of the player who already called. Twelve dollars is not much to show for your efforts and your pocket cowboys.

If you answered "raise three to five times the Big Blind," give yourself five points! This is the optimum play and here is why: You want some action with your premium pocket pair and you want to encourage weaker hands to call. With one caller I would raise to $20 or $25. This says little about the strength of your hand but lets players know you like your hand enough to bet it. Your ideal scenario is for a player with a good but not great Pre-Flop hand like QQ, JJ, TT, AK, AKs, KQ, AQ, or AJ to raise you back. If they do, your decision is easy because *you* then raise all-in and you are a favorite against all but aces.

If you do get called, what then? See Problem Two!

Problem Two: Cowboys, Part Two

Theme: Flop Play; Big Pairs

Stack Size: Small

Position: Middle

Continuation of Problem One: You raised to $25. Only the original caller is in early position, and the Button called. The pot is $87 (remember you posted) and you have $70 left in your stack. The Flop is:

The early position player checks. Do you:

- Bet $40?
- Check, hoping to check-raise?
- Bet your remaining stack?

If you answered bet $40, give yourself one point. This is really a continuation bet and is out of place here. The bet size is too small. It may give a straight or flush draw an incentive to call, as the player with a drawing hand is hoping to stack other players if they hit their card. Also what are you going to do if a player behind you raises? You have committed 70% of your total stack and over 50% of your Post-Flop stack. You are pot-committed. A fold to such a raise, therefore, is untenable as only pocket aces, two-pair, or a set beat you and you cannot really say with any certainty that your opponents have these holding, if you are raised.

If you answered check, hoping to check-raise, give yourself zero points. This is the type of play that may have merit in limit play but is useless in no-limit Hold'em. In limit play you would check-raise here in an effort to protect your hand, because you cannot bet enough to do so otherwise. Even in limit play with this Flop you must be certain that the player behind you is aggressive enough to bet if you check, because you do not want to give a free card, allowing either player a chance to outdraw you. *In no-limit Hold'em you make the most money when players call your big bets (or make big bets) with inferior hands to yours.* You do not need to trap here and may well trap yourself by trying to do so.

If you answered bet your remaining stack, give yourself five points. This is by far the best play. Your bet is less than the pot but, given your stack size, the most you can make. It is highly likely that your overpair is still the best hand and even if you are against two-pair or a set (very bad luck) you have outs. *When playing a small stack, you must bet your money fast when you have the advantage.*

If the Button is on a draw he is making a mistake by calling your bet because he cannot win enough of your stack to make his call profitable (you have nothing left) and he does not know if the early position player will call and give him sufficient pot odds. However, you will routinely get called by drawing hands in this situation, when the drawers have you covered. They reason that the Turn and River costs them nothing, since you cannot bet. This is true, but irrelevant because when they make their hand they cannot win any more money. In other words, they have neither the correct pot odds to call or the implied odds to make the call profitable. This type of thinking (on their part) comes from tournament play where they can try to knock you out for (it appears) little cost. This consideration is irrelevant in cash play because if you are outdrawn you merely re-load. *You have got the maximum amount of money in the pot when you have a clear advantage and that is the best you can do!*

Have you noticed how playing this way greatly simplifies your decisions when you have a short stack in no-limit Hold'em? You have effectively turned the game into one of two betting rounds and taken away the big stack's advantage, because you cannot now make any mistakes in the Turn and River.

Problem Three: Tight Is Right

Theme: Pre-Flop Hand Selection

Stack Size: Small

Position: Middle

Same game as in Problem Two! In the last hand the Button called and the early position player folded. The Button held A6 (spades) but did not improve and your kings held up. Since he had a stack of over $1,000 he did not seem that concerned. Your $100 has now grown to $227 and life feels good. In a euphoric state of reckless abandon you tip the dealer $2, so you now have a stack of $225.

You are still in middle position. An early-position player has raised to $20 and the player to your immediate right smooth calls the raise. Both players have stacks of over $600. The pot is $47. You look down to find you have:

Do you:

- Fold?
- Call?
- Re-raise all-in?
- Re-raise $150?

If you answered "call," give yourself zero points. Your hand plays badly against an early-position raiser who probably has you out-gunned. Even worse, the player to your right thinks it is worth a call and he may have you beaten too. Worse still, you may get popped in the back. Calling is a sure way to bleed money here.

If you answered "re-raise all-in," give yourself minus ten points. This is a TV poker move that may have its place under certain tournament conditions (pretty few, though) but is lame-brained here. You are risking you whole stack on a hand that is very likely to make second best or worse. Your bet is not going to drive out either the raiser or the caller if they have any sort of hand and from early position they are likely to have pretty good hands. You are risking a lot to make a little and are giving your opponents an easy call if they have a premium hand, and an easy fold if they were just playing about. Play like this and you will go broke fast in no-limit Hold'em.

If you answered "re-raise $150," give yourself minus five points. Not quite as lame-brained as the last choice but definitely a contender for the Poker Darwin Awards. In limit a re-raise here may have merit, if the aim is to get heads up with a loose player who will bet with inferior hands. Even in limit play a re-raise here would be a bad play because you have a raiser in early position and a caller in front of you. In no-limit this re-raise is terrible. AQ is a very marginal hand in no-limit play and has no place against early position raisers when *you* are in middle position. This re-raise does nothing except build a pot for those who have better hands than yours and pot-commits you. If you get re-raised, what are you going to do? The only merit is that you might be able to fold in the face of a re-raise. That is poor redemption.

If you answered "fold," give yourself five points. Now you get the idea! *You must tighten up your calling requirements a lot when you play NL Hold'em and there is a raise in front of you.* When you have a small stack (and you still do in relation to your opponents despite your last win) this is doubly true. No bet you make here will drive out a player with a decent hand and a big stack. You might call here with JJ, QQ, or maybe AKs but I don't much care for this play, even with these hands with a small stack in this situation. You are hoping to play the Flop cheaply and spike a set or, in the case of Aks, a flush and double through your bigger-stacked opponents. Mostly however you will miss the Flop and give yourself tough decisions on later streets. This type of loose Pre-Flop calling bleeds chips fast.

In this situation I would only play pocket aces or kings and then for a big raise (three to five times the pot), hoping to get all my money in as early as possible. Save your chips for a better situation. *When you play with a small stack you must play very tightly and selectively Pre-Flop if you want to show a profit.*

Problem Four: Small Pairs, Early Position

Theme: Pre-Flop Hand Selection

Stack Size: Small

Position: Early

You bought in for a little over the minimum and after two rounds you have not played a hand. You have just given up your second Small and Big Blinds and so are down $14. Your stack is just under $100. The players behind you seem pretty aggressive, and most pots have been two or three-handed, but no player has a stack over $700. You are under the gun and are dealt pocket fours. Do you:

- Call?
- Raise three times the Big Blind?
- Fold?

If you answered "call," give yourself one point. When you call here it is because you are hoping to flop a set to get a big payoff. It is very tempting to play all pairs in no-limit Hold'em from any position for a call or calling a small raise. However, to be profitable you really need the correct pot odds or implied odds. If you get lucky and nobody raises behind you, you may get to see the Flop cheaply, however from this position you leave yourself open to a raise. What will you do if you have to call $50 to see the Flop, once it comes back to you?

If you answered "raise," give yourself zero points. This is not a raising hand from early position, especially with a small stack. Your raise is effectively a semi-bluff Pre-Flop. Your hand is just not strong enough to make a credible raise.

If you answered "fold," give yourself five points. When playing a small stack you must be very selective of the hands you play from early position and with aggressive players behind you, you need to play a hand that can stand some heat. Under the gun your minimum starting pocket pair should be TT and AK. Even AQs is not strong enough to play from here. Playing less tightly will bleed chips.

Problem Five: Premium Pairs Pre-Flop

Theme: Pre-Flop Hand Selection

Stack Size: Small

Position: Button

You have yet to play a hand since you are playing ultra tight and the Blinds have passed you three times. You still have $130 in your stack as you bought in for a little more than the minimum, but players with bigger stacks have been making comments about your micro-stack and goading you to buy in for the maximum. Your poker manhood (or womanhood) is not offended because you know you are playing correctly. A player in early position has called. An aggressive player in middle position, with a stack of about $750, has raised to $15 and the rest have folded. The pot stands at $27. You peek at your cards and are happy to find:

Do you:

- Call the raise?
- Raise all-in?
- Re-raise to $40–$50?

If you answered "call," give yourself one point. Calling here is really slowplaying Pre-Flop, a strategy I am not a big fan of. The objective is to encourage weaker hands to call then spring a trap when they bet the Flop. The problem is that either you allow a mediocre hand to get away too cheaply, or you find yourself trapped if someone flops a big hand.

If you answered "raise all-in," give yourself two points. You are getting closer to the right idea, but this blunderbuss raise will cause most players just to fold. By making this move, you have pretty clearly stated that you have a very strong hand, especially as your play up to now has been tight.

If you answered "raise to $40–$50," reward yourself with five points. This is more to the point. Remember your objective is to get players with weaker hands (everybody except another pair of aces) to call. To maximize their mistake you want them to call as much as possible. A bet of this size is likely to get called by the raiser and even by the early caller. This raise announces a strong hand but still leaves some doubt as to what you have. If you get raised back, of course you move all-in with your remaining stack. If you get called, you will probably move in on the Flop, thus you've got your money in early when you are likely to be leading. About the only time I would not move all-in on the Flop here is if the Flop is single suited and I have no ace of that suit or the Flop comes K,Q, J or K, Q, T. In the latter instance the likelihood of being against a set or two-pair is very great so if the Flop is checked to me, I would check too hoping to improve on the Turn. If someone does set you all-in on this type of Flop, it is hard to get away from the overpair. If you know your opponent is likely to show strength only with two-pair and above, you could fold. However with a short stack a call is not a mistake here, even if you think that there is a 30 percent chance that you are against two-pair, because you are beating everything except a made hand and you have chances to improve too.

If the Flop is single suited and there is a call and an over-call or a raise and you do not hold the ace of that suit in your hand a fold is usually wise. You are probably looking at one flush at least, and you may be almost drawing dead.

Here, though, the rule is *to make the largest bet you think your opponent will call when you have an advantage.* Again you are attempting to get as much of your money in as soon as reasonably possible when you have the lead. This is a simple, strong, and almost unbeatable play against opponents who play too loosely. You will find scores of such players in games like this and they make an ultra-tight, small-stack strategy profitable.

Problem Six: Getting Re-Raised

Theme: Moving All-In

Stack Size: Small

Position: Cut-Off

You started with $100 but have lost a pot and paying Blinds has eaten your stack. You have $60 left. Every player has you covered. One player from middle position has called and the rest have folded. The Button is reasonably aggressive and the Blinds seem a little loose. You look down to find:

You raise the pot to $15 and the Button re-raises you to $30—the minimum raise. The Small Blind folds but the Big Blind calls $30. The original middle-position caller folds. The pot stands at $77 and you have $45 left. The Big Blind has you covered too. Do you:

- Move all-in?
- Fold?
- Call?

If you answered "fold," score zero points. Some players will argue that the action has told them that they are up against aces or kings and therefore they are saving money. Mostly, however, you cannot put a player on a particular hand but only on a *range of possible hands*. It is quite possible that one of the other players has a pair of aces or kings but they could also have pocket jacks, tens, or nines (even queens) also. They may have AKs, AQs, AK, AQ, AJs, AJ, KQs, or KQ. It is certainly possible that they hold hands inferior to these, since when playing against a small stack many players will take a shot at the little guy, figuring that they can only lose a little. Of course, that is bad poker thinking. The re-raises mean little here and you may still have the best hand.

If you answered "call," score two points. At least you are still in the pot here but what is your objective? The ideal situation would be to be heads up against a player with a lower pair or perhaps AJ or KQ. It may be the case that the remaining players are now really aiming to play a side pot bigger than the main pot against each other. You have a chance to get your money in when you probably have both players beaten. With a larger stack you may want to call and see the texture of the Flop. Here your call leaves you with only $15 and you are pot-committed.

If you answered "move all-in," score five points. Yes, given the theme it was not hard to guess that going all-in here is the best move. Let's look at the decision more closely. The answer is based on bet size and stack size. The larger the ratio between your initial bet and your remaining stack, the stronger the hand you need to move all-in. Here you bet $15 leaving you $45 in your stack, a 3:1 ratio. Your hand is plenty strong enough to move all-in. You have the third best starting hand in Hold'em so moving all-in here gives you the strongest chance of doubling or even tripling up. In fact, even with a hand as weak as pocket nines and certainly a hand like AK, you could safely move all-in in this spot. Your opponents can win no more money from you in later rounds and you have got your money in when you probably have the best of it, and still have chances in the event that you do not. That is about as much as you can do in poker.

Problem Seven: It Ain't Always So Easy!

Theme: Flop Play

Stack Size: Smallish!

Position: Middle

You have picked off a small pot and now have a stack of $115. The Blinds are $1 and $2. You look down and see:

You don't mind a little action with a hand this strong, but the table has been playing loosely and you don't want to play against five or more callers. Ideally you want to play this hand heads up, but in this type of game with loose Pre-Flop action this is hard to do. A very large bet will tend to chase players away. Two players in front limp from early position. You make it $15 to go. The Button and the Big Blind both call the raise as does one of the early-position players, but the other early-position player folds. The pot is four-handed. There is $63 in the pot. You have $100 left. All three players have you covered.

The Flop comes as shown on page 60:

The two players in front both check and the action is on you. Do you:

- Check?
- Bet $15?
- Bet $30–$45?
- Move all-in?

The first thing you should notice is that as your stack size increases (in relation to the Blinds and bets) your decisions become more complex. One objective of the small-stack, no-limit game is to simplify your decisions, but as your stack grows even by a small amount, this becomes more difficult.

If you answered "check," score one point. This is not terrible play but it's pretty wimpy. You are practically asking the player behind you to steal the pot. In no-limit games of this size, players with any sort of hand will tend to bet, unless they have a monster and then they will try to trap. By checking here you are hoping that the Button will check and you can pick up something on the Turn. You are giving the initiative to other players and effectively telling the table the Flop has missed you. Also, what will you do in the face of a bet from the Button?

If you answered "bet $15," score zero points. This play is worse than the last! This type of bet is typical of small-stakes no-limit games (where players often have little understanding of bet size) and really does nothing except bleed chips or lessen win rates. The bet is too small to chase out any flush draws and if called around, actually gives the drawing player the correct pot odds to call. If any players are trapping with a five they will probably call and wait for the Turn. Again, how will you react to a bet or a check on the Turn, especially if you make a pair? A bet of this type more or less announces that you have a weak hand but are making a "cheap" bet to see if you can steal a pot. Players with any sort of hand will raise here, you will probably have to fold, and you have just lost $15 for nothing.

If you answered "move all-in," score three points. This is not such a bad play and some poker experts would argue that it is the best play. Certainly by moving all-in here you cannot make any further mistakes and you have put the question to the other players. It is hard for a player to call this bet without a pretty strong hand. My problem with this play is that you are betting $100 to win $63. Since all of your opponents have you covered, players with even a moderate hand might look you up to keep you honest and perhaps get an insight into your play. You may have the best hand here, but you could also be far behind. You actually make it easy for your opponents to avoid mistakes: If they have a strong hand they will call, if they have a weak hand they will fold. You will cause them to play correctly in either event. If your remaining stack had been the size of the pot or less, moving all-in would have been the correct play, but stack size alters how you play in no-limit Hold'em.

If you answered "bet $30–$45," score five points. This looks like the best play to me and here is why: Your opponents know that you probably have a strong hand as you were prepared to raise early callers in middle position. From their perspective you may be holding any pair from TT to AA or two big cards. A continuation bet here of about a half to three quarters of the pot should get the job done. If you get called then you are probably beaten and can check the Turn. Any flush draws cannot profitably call this bet and they have neither pot odds nor implied odds, since after this bet you will only have between $70 and $55 left depending on the size of your Flop bet. Your bet here really gives no information about your hand. You may be betting two big unpaired cards, but you may also have an overpair, AQ, or even a set of queens. A bet of this type may get hands like KQ, QJ, or QT to fold and make it very hard for even JJ or TT to continue.

Here you *really* put the question to your opponents and make mistakes on their part much more likely. If you do get a call you may get a free card on the Turn and even River and an ace, king, or back door flush could bring in the bacon. Conversely if you are raised or even get a call you have no need to continue stabbing at the pot. You have bet enough to foster a variety of possible mistakes and you are betting $30 to $45 to win $63. If your opponents fold, you have done very nicely with this semi-bluff. Why do I say bet $30 to $45 rather than suggest a specific sum? There are two reasons: First, you should vary the amount of your continuation bets so that your opponents do not know if you are betting with, say, top pair, an even better hand, or bluffing, thus your opponents remain confused and mistake-prone. Second, in some games $30 will get the job done and in others you will need to bet $45. You base the figure on the flavor of your game and the observation of your opponents. When making this type of play *bet enough to get the job done and no more.* This is why observing how your opponents play is very important in no-limit Hold'em.

Problem Eight: Nut Sellers, Part One

Theme: Flop Play Against Very Tight Players

Stack Size: Medium

Position: Button

You have been seated at a table with a number of very tight players. At least two of them seem only willing to play the nuts or close to it in any given situation. You have stolen a lot of small pots from these players and by targeting them have gradually increased your stack to $350. You bought in for $200. One of the Nut Sellers has been complaining about your "wild play" and keeps mumbling about "when he gets a real hand, then…" On the Button you pick up:

There are three players in the pot when it gets to you, including the super tight player who has been complaining about your play. The player under the gun put in a small raise (total of $6) and the Nut Seller to his right called, as did a player in middle position. There is $18 in the pot plus the Blinds for a total of $21. The action is on you and you decide to raise with your AK. You make it $30 to go. Both Blinds fold and the player under the gun folds. To your surprise the Nut Seller calls but the player in middle position folds. The pot holds $75 and will now be contested heads up. "Just me and the best hand," you joke, and the Nut Seller grunts in response.

The Flop is:

The Nut Seller looks pained and quickly checks but something feels wrong to you. You have top-pair and there is only a diamond draw and possibly straight draws too. Do you:

• Bet the pot?
• Check?
• Bet between one third and half the pot?

If you answered "bet the pot," give yourself two points. You have top pair but is it really necessary to bet so much? A very tight player will normally fold to almost any bet that does not give him profitable pot odds or if he does not already have a very strong hand. Your bet allows him to get away from the hand easily and costs you too much if he is trapping with a monster.

If you answered "check," give yourself zero points. If you check here you have the spine of a limp tea cloth. You have position, you have top-pair, and you are heads up. You cannot always be waiting for the nuts. Checking serves no purpose whatsoever and with the diamonds out there giving a free draw to the flush, checking is a no-no. Your opponent has shown no strength. You must bet to try and win the pot.

If you answered "bet one third to one half of the pot," score five points. This is plenty to get the job done against a tight and predictable player. Unless he has a very good hand, he is unlikely to give you any action. Just don't bet too little and give him the odds for a draw. Remember this is still a small pot and you want to keep it that way with one pair against a tight and predictable player like this. *Don't play big pots against Nut Sellers unless you have the nuts!*

Problem Nine: Nut Sellers, Part Two

Theme: Turn and River Against Very Tight Players

Stack Size: Medium

Position: Button

This problem continues on from Problem Eight. You decided to bet thirty dollars on the Flop with top-pair and a king kicker. To your surprise the Nut Seller smooth calls. The only time you have seen him call a Flop bet was with a set and a straight draw on a rainbow board with five other callers. Something is rotten in the state of Denmark!

The Turn card is:

Again, after a very brief pause the Nut Seller checks. This card seems to be harmless to you but you cannot figure out why the Nut Seller called your bet on the Flop. If you check you are allowing a free draw to a diamond flush so you want to bet, but how much? Perhaps a shot from the other barrel will knock him out of the pot but just as you are about to put chips in the pot you notice that the Nut Seller's fingers are twitching very slightly. Against reason, it seems, you check.

The River is:

After a pause the Nut Seller bets $100. Do you:

- Come over the top and move all-in?
- Call?
- Fold?

If you answered "move all-in," score minus five points. You have not taken into account the type of player you are against. Everything is screaming at you that this player has a hand he likes. Players like this will only lead out when they have a very strong hand. Clearly this player wants you to call. The check on the Turn was an attempt to trap you. If you had bet, my guess is that the trap

would have been sprung on the Turn and your bet would have
been raised. Since the Nut Seller wants a decent payoff, the bet here
is a somewhat desperate attempt to get a call. Your opponent has
made a fairly basic mistake, though, in betting an amount you are
unlikely to call. Moving all-in is likely to cost you your whole stack
here, as you are probably up against a full house. The Nut Seller almost certainly called with TT Pre-Flop, and made a set on the Flop.
Again, this very tight, risk-averse type of player rarely continues
without having a strong hand. The call on the Flop should have
caused warning bells to ring in your head. Your bet won't scare him
off, and he is not bluffing with a medium-strength hand. He knows
you must have something as you raised Pre-Flop and bet the Flop.
Despite all of this he clearly wants a call.

If you answered "call," score zero points. Okay, I am being gen-
erous here and awarding you zero. This highlights a major difference between limit and no-limit Hold'em: In limit Hold'em, a call
would have been correct here because you are risking a big bet
(only double the size of the small bet) to win a large pot and therefore your call is profitable long-term, because you only have to be
correct a small percentage of the time to have positive expectation.
Of course, this is a whole artificial consideration because you
would not have a pot of this size in a limit game where the Blinds
were so small. Even a 5–10 game would not have you looking at a
pot of this size with the action as given. However, the point is that
here you are risking $100 to win $175 and you only have two-pair
(aces and sevens) with a king kicker. Against a wild, loose, or tricky
opponent this call may be justified, but here you are just throwing
your money away. This player is not going to risk his $100 plus a
possible raise from you without a very strong hand. In no-limit
Hold'em, a pair at the Turn or at the River (or even aces up as here)
is not much of a hand, in the face of heavy action from a conservative and predictable opponent.

If you answered "fold," score five points. This is an easy fold in
no-limit Hold'em. You raised Pre-Flop and you made a decent-
sized bet on the Flop. If you cannot shake a Nut Seller off, you are

just about certain to be behind. The $100 River bet is a cast-iron indication that your opponent is not fooling around. The calls Pre-Flop and on the Flop and the check on the Turn no longer enter into the equation. The latest action is the most significant. Players of this type bluffing on the end is as rare as snow in August so you are not facing a bluff. The only question is whether you have the best hand at the showdown. I think you know what my answer is to that one. The golden rule with Nut Sellers is *steal small pots from them and refuse to play big pots against them unless you have the nuts or something very close to the nuts.* Anything else is likely to cause you serious trip drainage as you attempt to play big pots against Nut Sellers with mediocre hands.

Problem Ten: Big Hands, Big Pots

Theme: Making the Most of Big Hands

Stack Size: Medium

Position: Big Blind

The game is $1–$2 with a maximum buy-in of $300. You have been steadily making money winning a few decent pots and have built your stack to $500 (a medium-size stack for this level), having bought in for $200. You look down to see that you have:

You would be happy if you got to check your option. The game thus far has been fairly conservative with a couple of loose players making the game profitable. A player who seems to play fairly well, raises in middle position to $10. The Button (one of the loose and fairly aggressive players) calls the raise. Both players have stacks about equal to your own so calling an additional $8 to win what could be a big pot, if you hit your hand, seems like a risk worth taking, and you in fact call, after the Small Blind folds. The pot is three-handed and contains $31. Your opponents both have position on you.

The Flop is:

You hit your card and are willing to play a big pot because you have a strong (though, of course, not unbeatable) hand and a good chance of doubling through your opponents.

Being first to act, the action is on you. Do you:

- Bet $30?
- Check and call?
- Check and raise if there is a bet?
- Bet $50?

The following answers will demonstrate that we are into the more complex thinking that no-limit Hold'em demands as the stacks get deeper. It also demonstrates that there is not absolutely one best way to play in any given no-limit Hold'em scenario.

If you answered "bet $30," score five points. The key to this bet size is to think about what you are trying to achieve. What you want to do is get your whole stack in the middle and you want it there as fast as possible but no faster! *The key lesson here is that big hands are meant to play for big pots!* Here, you have such a hand. Now, you may well argue that you have a big hand but your opponents may have a set of kings or a set of nines. In that case you are destined to lose your whole stack and there is nothing you can do about it. In a game of medium stacks you are likely to lose your whole stack if you have an under set or if your opponent outdraws you. However, if the stacks were much deeper, say ten times the size they are in this example, this would not be true, because you would be unlikely to call such large bets without the nuts. In this case, you will lose your stack if for example your opponent has two-pair or a flush draw and gets lucky and makes a full house or a flush, and you do not improve.

The first thing to assume is that at least one of your opponents (or ideally both) has a hand that is strong enough that they are willing to commit their whole stack. Obviously this is likely to be a fairly strong hand. If your opponents hold AQ or AJ or even a pair of tens or jacks you are unlikely to get action, no matter what you bet. Your opponents will simply fold. You are looking for opponents who will commit with, say, top pair, a draw, or ideally two-pair, which is a hard hand to get away from in no-limit Hold'em with stacks this size. So then the question is how do you get them to commit their chips? The answer is, a little at a time. Of course, if your opponents put *you* all-in you can just call and your work is done, but against conservative players this is unlikely. Instead you should think about what bet you hope to make on the Turn or River and see how you can get there without arousing the suspicion of your opponents and instead make them believe that beyond a certain point, they are pot-committed.

By betting $30 here you are hoping that at least one of your opponents will raise, allowing you to either re-raise now or make a larger bet, say $100 to $150 on the Turn, and bet the rest of your stack on the River, if the pot is still being contested. If neither opponent raises but rather calls, you can still make a pot-sized bet of a decent size on the Turn and without arousing too much suspicion. Then if either opponent is slowplaying two-pair or making a semi-bluff with a flush draw and raises *you*, you can set them all in. If they call because they feel pot-committed you have achieved your objective.

Now, of course there are a lot of possibilities along the highways and byways of this hand, but at least by playing this way you have set yourself a clear road map and a clear objective of maximizing your potential profit. Remember, only opponents with decent hands will play against you, so you only have to consider players who have such a hand in determining your strategy.

If you answered "check and call," score two points. The extended slowplay is one way of playing here but probably not best. For example, say the first opponent bets $20 and the other calls and you call. There is now $91 in the pot. What do you do on the Turn? If a diamond comes can you bet out when there is now a strong possibility that one player has made a flush? You are now effectively semi-bluffing. If a blank hits do you bet hoping to induce calls or check and spring your trap on the Turn? If you check the Turn you could easily give a free card. Do you maximize your chances of winning a big pot by this check and call strategy?

If you answered "check and raise," score one point. This is a fairly standard beginner's attempt at a trap; slowplay with a big hand and then pounce like a rabid beast on the Flop. The problem with this is that it is pretty obvious that you have a big hand when you play this way, as you are willing to check-raise two opponents. Also you are allowing your opponents to control the betting at this point and this is not ideal. Remember, you want to get as much of your money in the middle as possible when you have a big hand like this. Does a check-raise get the job done here? No. It allows either or probably both players to fold and lose a minimal amount. For example, let's say you check, the player in middle position checks, and the Button bets $15. If you then raise and make it, say, $50 on top, it is pretty easy for either player to get away from his hand. Likewise if the player in middle position bets, say, $30 and the Button calls and you raise to $60 or $100 (or more) it is pretty easy for either player to get away from a moderate hand like AK or a flush draw. The result is that you have not gotten much of a pay-off.

If you answered "bet $50," score three points. It is hard to criticize this bet too much except in two respects: First, by over-betting the pot you may chase out a player holding top pair or a drawing hand, if the players are conservative. However, you will not discourage two-pair or possibly even AK. Second, this bet amount may discourage the looser player on the Button from putting in a bullying type of raise because your willingness to bet such a large amount on the Flop with two players behind, indicates you like your hand. The net result may be that the bet discourages any further action.

Conversely, if this bet *is* called and you make a pot-sized bet on the Turn, it will be very hard for either opponent to determine the true strength of your hand. In fact, it could be argued that this type of over-strong betting makes it look like you have a weaker hand than you in fact have and are betting to discourage any callers. If you think that your opponents think *you* have top pair and they think you think *they* have a draw, they may well expect you to play top pair this way.

Here it is obvious that there is no one correct play and your bet size depends on how your opponents play and what you believe they think of how *you* play. Despite this there are clearly some wrong ways to play the hand and you will constantly see these errors at these limits. The key point to grasp in this problem is that *when you have made a big hand you want your opponents to pay-off as much as possible and you must construct a situation so that they almost have to continue in the pot.* You want them to make as big and as costly an error as possible. Of course, you must be lucky enough that they have some sort of hand to play with or else however you play, you will get little or no action.

Problem Eleven: Small Blind Sorrows

Theme: Starting Hands

Stack Size: Large

Position: Small Blind

You are playing in a $1–$2 game with a maximum buy-in of $200 and have been doing very well. The game is passive and loose with lots of Pre-Flop calling. A number of players have busted out and after playing for a few hours you have built your stack to $900 from your initial buy-in of $100. In fact, you now have the largest stack on the table with one other stack around $600 and the rest ranging from $60 to $400.

You are in the Small Blind and look down to find:

There are five callers, including the Button, with only the Big Blind yet to act. Normally you would muck this hand without a second thought but the pot already has $13 (including Blind money). You have to put in only one dollar to call. Do you:

- Call?
- Raise?
- Fold?

If you answered "call," give yourself zero points. Many players believe that tossing in a dollar in these circumstances is not a bad gamble. This is a fallacy. It looks like you are getting fantastic odds

(13:1) and almost any two cards become playable. Thinking like this is why most players play too loosely from the Blinds, especially the Small Blind. Not only do many players make poor starting hand selections from the Small Blind, but if they catch a piece of the Flop, they then face difficult decisions from a weak position for the rest of the hand. The likelihood of compounding these mistakes becomes greater than the potential gain from a miracle Flop. If you play one hundred hands at a ten-handed table, you will save five Big Blinds (potentially a lot more if you play badly beyond the Flop) by tightening up your starting hand requirements from the Small Blind. Stop the bleeding!

If you answered "raise," give yourself minus five points. This is a terrible play, but I have seen players with large stacks make raises in this type of situation with unpaired, unconnected, and unsuited pocket cards. Why? Well, they argue that because you have a large stack you can bully a passive table playing this way, plus if you get lucky and flop two-pair or trips, your hand is very well disguised, and you can take down a big pot. We will examine the probability of these events occurring in the next paragraph but before that there are three other lessons to be learned: The first is that a big stack is not a license for loose and sloppy play. *If everyone else has a small or medium stack, you are still playing small- and medium-stack poker.* Cash is not like a tournament where you can use a big stack to intimidate players and knock them out of the game altogether. The second lesson is that you must take account of your position. Here you are raising in the worst possible position for subsequent betting rounds. The third lesson is that even in the Small Blind, you still have to select your starting hands with care. Raising here is tantamount to giving your money away.

If you answered fold, give yourself five points. Well done if you mucked this piece of trash, but do you know why? If you are tempted to play this type of hand it may be because you are hoping for a big payout if you flop two-pair. The odds of hitting two-pair on the Flop is a smidgen better than 28:1, however. You certainly do not have the pot odds to make this play, and you just about never have the implied odds to do so either. Here, as the big stack at the table, you definitely do *not* have the implied odds. In fact, the probability of missing the Flop entirely is 0.68, so even picking up a piece of the Flop is unlikely. If in doubt a good rule of thumb is not to play a hand from the Small Blind if you would not be willing to play that same hand from middle position. This change alone can make a significant improvement to your overall win rate.

Problem Twelve: Small Blind Joy

Theme: Starting Hands

Stack Size: Large

Position: Small Blind

This is the same $1–$2 game as Problem Eleven. The table remains fairly passive but you have not had a playable hand in the last circuit. There are six callers before the action gets to you, including the Cut-Off and the Button. The pot contains $15. The player in the Big Blind has been passive too, checking hands and not raising from the Big Blind. You look down to find:

Do you:

- Call?
- Raise?
- Fold?

If you answered "call," give yourself five points. This seems similar to the last problem in that you have unconnected, unpaired cards but the fact that you hold a *suited ace* makes a big difference. Your approximate odds of making flush by the River are 14.63:1 with *suited but unconnected cards as is the case here*. If you make a flush with this hand, however, it is likely to be the nut flush, if the Board offers no straight flush possibilities. Additionally, your ace means that if you flop two-pair, it is likely to be *top* two pair or at least of course aces up. In a passive game like this you could even make a play at the pot if you flop top-pair, and lead out on the Flop, assuming that your observation of your opponents has indicated that they will fold hands to a decent-sized bet on the Flop or merely call in the face of strong betting, allowing you to play this hand cheaply to the River where at the showdown it may well be the best hand, even with a poor kicker such as a seven. This combination of factors make this a playable hand here and one that you would be glad to play.

If you answered "raise," give yourself zero points. It could be argued that raising in this scenario makes some sense in limit play where you then build a larger pot when other players call your raise. Then if you flop a flush or flush draw, you may be playing for a large pot. However, apart from the possibility of a re-raise, you remain out of position for the rest of the hand and even in limit Hold'em this makes it a doubtful play. In no-limit Hold'em a raise here may well attract a re-raise and you have effectively played yourself out of a potentially lucrative pot. There is no need to attempt to build a pot here because if you flop a flush, two-pair, or a draw, there is a good chance that one of the other limpers will lead in the betting if you check, or call if you choose to bet out.

If you answered "fold," give yourself minus five points. This is too conservative. It is true that you are out of position but you have a chance of making or drawing to the nut flush with a favorable Flop. In a passive game such as this, these types of drawing hands may be your best opportunity for a decent win, especially if your opponents are regularly drawing to small flushes, or calling to the showdown with cards like top-pair, weak kicker.

Problem Thirteen: But They're Suited!

Theme: Suited Connectors Raised Pots

Stack Size: Medium

Position: Middle

You find yourself in a game with a mixture of loose players and tighter, but aggressive players. You have built your stack to $350 from an initial buy-in of $200. One of the looser players in middle position opens for a raise of $12. You estimate his stack to be about $150. The players after him fold but one of the tighter but more aggressive players sitting just to your right (whose stack stands at about $700) re-raises, making it $30 to go. You are next to act and you look down to see:

Do you:

- Call?
- Fold?
- Raise?

If you answered "call," score zero points. Your hand has definite possibilities but not here. The looser player may be raising in early position with less than premium values and the solid player next to you may be attempting to raise so as to isolate the loose, early-position raiser. For this reason, his re-raise may not indicate a powerhouse hand either, but then again this line of thinking could be entirely wrong. There is a good chance that one or even both players have superior hands and your drawing hand is not one that you want to be playing in a raised pot.

If you answered "fold," score five points. This hand is not meant for this type of situation. This looks like things are building to a big pot and *you do not have a hand to play a big pot with.* You could argue that a hand only ever becomes big on the Flop and beyond, and whilst there is some truth in this viewpoint, this type of hand needs players *and* small Pre-Flop bets to become playable. This hand may indeed become a big hand, but if you routinely play hands like this in pots that are raised Pre-Flop, you are going to bleed a lot of chips. Most Flops will not hit you and you are going to have to give up the hand on the Flop. Added to this is the fact that in middle position there may be a raise behind you. The flavor of this game and the specifics of this situation mean that you should pass and wait for better opportunities.

If you answered "raise," score minus five points. What are you thinking? Your hand is beaten by at least one player and probably both. Your positional advantage cannot overcome what is almost certain to be the worst hand. This is not a raising situation.

Problem Fourteen: They're Suited, They Really Are!

Theme: Starting Hands

Stack Size: Medium

Position: Cut-Off

You are at a $1–$2 table with a $100 minimum and $300 maximum buy-in. You have been playing at this table for over three hours and won a few pots. You bought in for $100 and now have $350. The game conditions are pretty good. You are sitting to the immediate left of a loose and aggressive player who likes to play lots of hands for a raise. The players behind you are fairly tight but passive. A player in early position with a stack of about $400 limps and so does another player whose stack is about $350. The aggressive player to your right who has had some erratic swings in his fortune is distracted by the sandwich he just ordered arriving via a casino waitress and folds. You look down to find:

The players behind you have been passive and no player has a stack smaller than $200 or larger than $500. Do you:

- Fold?
- Call?
- Raise three to five times the Big Blind?

If you answered "fold," give yourself one point. This is very tight play in this situation, but as you are in middle position, it could be argued that players will raise and re-raise behind you, driving you out of the pot. Middle position is not the best place from which to play this hand in a no-limit game. However, I feel that this play is excessively conservative given the fact that game conditions are fairly passive. If there were looser or very aggressive players behind you, then a fold may well be the best play. You must pay attention to game conditions to determine the suitability of a particular play in a specific situation.

If you answered "call," give yourself five points. When you have suited connectors, as here, your odds of getting a straight or flush by the River are approximately 4.44:1. Therefore in pots with three or more limpers these hands have a positive expectation Pre-Flop. However, this assumes that you are going to get to the River. In a passive game with loose players, which is usually the most profitable type of game to play in, these hands become playable. In this type of game you probably will have to hit your hand to win the pot and there is a good likelihood that the pot will only be won by showing down the best hand. In later problems we'll examine exactly how you play draws in no-limit Hold'em on the Flop and beyond. The thing to understand here is that in this situation you can usually profitably call Pre-Flop. Ideally you would want other players to limp behind you, improving your odds so that you can see the Flop cheaply and determine on the Flop whether you will play on. The single danger here is that the pot will be raised and re-raised behind you. If so, you will probably be better off folding Pre-Flop, because you will have lost the implied odds that make suited connectors profitable in no-limit play. Remember, if you call with this hand it is okay to dump it Pre-Flop if the action becomes too heavy. This is quite different from limit play where a raise from a player in late position, when there have been many callers, should usually be called for a single bet when the action gets back to you. The important thing to understand is that if you continue after the Flop, it is because you are probably on a flush or straight draw with this hand.

If you answered "raise," give yourself minus five points. This is not a raising situation. You may get re-raised and will then have to dump the hand. Here you want to see the Flop as cheaply as possible. Your hand plays better against multiple opponents and you do not want to thin the field. You want to encourage callers. In *late* position a hand like this is often raised for value in limit Hold'em when there are many callers ahead of you. This can be a very effective play in limit Hold'em but is usually counter-productive in no-limit Hold'em where players have the option to bet any amount. If you face a heavy re-raise you have played yourself out of the pot. In no-limit Hold'em you must select your hands, and especially your raising hands, carefully. If a player puts in a small raise behind you in this scenario after you have called, you can probably call the raise if it is not too large, there are at least three other callers, and each caller has a stack as big as or bigger than your own. You must also play on the Flop and beyond well, of course. Position is even more important in no-limit than limit Hold'em, and loose raising is more costly than even loose calling.

Problem Fifteen: Small Pairs

Theme: Starting Hands

Stack Size: Medium/Large

Position: Early

You are in a $2–$5 game with a minimum buy-in of $100 and a maximum of $500. You bought in for the minimum, but you have observed that a number of your opponents are loose and a little aggressive but not hyper-aggressive. You have won a few pots and you believe that to get a decent shot at the loose money you need a bigger stack so you have topped up and now have $500 in your stack. The stacks vary in size but two players who appear to be amongst the loosest at the table have you covered. In this game there is often a raise with three to five callers Pre-Flop. You are in early position. The player to your right who is under the gun calls. There is $12 in the pot. You look down to find that you hold the cards pictured opposite:

Do you:

- Raise 3-5 times the Big Blind?
- Fold?
- Call?

If you answered "raise," give yourself minus five points. This is not a raising hand from early position. You are primarily looking to win the pot by hitting a set on the Flop and a raise here will only attract action from superior hands. You are looking for big implied odds with this hand so anybody calling this raise is likely to have you beaten from the start. Even if they call with high unpaired cards the chances that the Flop will be non-paired and not dangerous, that is, contain overcards or flush or straight draws, is very low. No raising here!

If you answered "fold," give yourself one point. I give one point for this very tight play. If you are expecting hot and heavy action behind, then small pairs become non-playable in early position so this very tight play has its place. Here however, the players behind are not hyper-aggressive and if you want a shot at the stacks of the loosest players this is the type of hand you are looking for. Folding here is inappropriate to game conditions.

If you answered "call," give yourself five points. This is the optimal play. You know what you want from the start and that is to flop a set. It is unlikely that the pot will be won any other way. If you do flop a set your hand is well disguised and you stand a good chance of taking down a decent pot if one or more of your opponents Flops a hand such as top-pair, a draw, or two-pair. If you do not flop a set then you will almost certainly be folding if there is any action because your position does not allow for any bluffing opportunities in later rounds. Here you call hoping that others will limp. If there is a small raise in late position you are happy to call that raise, if you believe it probable that others will do the same. You risk being raised and re-raised Pre-Flop here, but if you are, you can always dump the hand losing only the $5 you put into the pot here. Strictly speaking, you need to have eight callers Pre-Flop to have the correct pot odds for this play. Of course, this is a rare occurrence. If you get four callers or more though that is fine assuming the callers have big stacks. Why? Implied odds again. A hand that is well disguised, such as a set, figures to get decent action on the Flop and beyond, because it will be hard for players with top-pair and a decent kicker to get away from their hand.

So what sort of implied odds make small pairs like this playable in this type of situation? Your stack should be at least fifteen times the Big Blind and, of course, so should your opponents'. These should really be your minimum requirements in my opinion. Personally I prefer to see my stacks of twenty times the Big Blind at least. In this game that is only $100, so we are comfortable in calling here. The next problem continues with this same hand.

Problem Sixteen: Small Pairs to Sets

Theme: Playing Sets

Stack Size: Medium/Large

Position: Early

Well, things have not turned out exactly as you would like because the player to your right raised to $15. He has a stack of $700. However, this being a loose table the raiser gets three callers! This is not an uncommon situation in small no-limit Hold'em games. The limpers are hoping to hit the Flop and are willing to risk a little for the chance to win a big pot. The Small Blind folds but the Big Blind calls. The original caller to your right calls too. The action is on you again. There are five players in the hand and the pot stands at $82. Each limper has a stack of at least $200. Do you:

- Call?
- Raise?
- Fold?

If you answered "call," give yourself five points. This is the correct play. You have to call $15 in a pot that stands at $82, and your odds are 5.46:1. On strict pot odds this is not quite enough. You are looking for odds of 7.5:1 or more. Do you have them? Yes, again because of the *implied odds*. If you hit your set it is almost a certainty that one of the other players will either bet, allowing you to raise; or call, playing a trapping move; or even raise your bet. Implied odds always involve an element of guesswork on your part, but if you flop a set of eights it will be exceptionally well disguised and therefore will get action from loose players like this, who all have stacks of more than ten times the raise. Also, the raise Pre-Flop usually indicates the likelihood of strong action on the Flop. The Pre-Flop raiser is likely to make a *continuation bet*, even if he misses the Flop and one or more players are likely to call. You could probably check the Flop if you hit your set and still be okay. Finally, notice that your call closes the betting action for this round. You cannot be forced out of the pot by a raise. This call is an opportunity to win a big pot if the Flop is kind. These are the sort of opportunities that make a substantial contribution to your profit in no-limit Hold'em.

If you answered "raise," give yourself minus five points. Raising here is misplaced aggression. If the original raiser pops you back with a substantial raise and the other players are caught between you, then they may all fold. You would now face calling a big bet with what is almost certainly the worst hand (or at best a marginally better hand if the raiser has, say, AK), and the raiser has position on you allowing him to dictate the action. If you do not flop a set you would be in trouble here. You do not want to re-open the betting in this scenario, but you do want to see the Flop.

If you answered "fold," give yourself zero points. Just because the pot has been raised Pre-Flop does not mean that small pairs become automatically unplayable. You must look at the specifics of each situation to determine if the hand is playable. This is why it is not realistic to give blanket rules such as, "Never play small pairs Pre-Flop in early position if the pot is raised." No-limit Hold'em does not lend itself to rules like this.

This hand is continued in the next problem!

Problem Seventeen: Sets on the Flop

Theme: Big Hands on the Flop

Stack Size: Medium/Large

Position: Early

This continues the same game from Problem Sixteen. It has happened. You have a favorable Flop. Here it is:

You have flopped a big hand, a set of eights, and are willing to play a big pot. The only hand that can be beating yours right now is a pair of jacks. Is it possible that one of your opponents holds this hand? Yes. However, this is only one of a range of possible hands that they could hold and you cannot live in fear of being against the nut hand all the time. If they do hold jacks you are destined to probably lose your whole stack and there is little you can do about it. Against all other hands, though, you are in a commanding position and now you have to consider how to make the most out of this situation. Notice that with this Flop several straight and flush draws are possible so you are not out of the woods yet. You must play correctly on the Flop and beyond to make the most of a favorable situation. To your surprise the player to your left bets $20 into the $97 pot. The original raiser is to your immediate left and as you glance at him he seems to be reaching for chips. Do you:

- Call?
- Raise $80–$100?
- Raise all-in?
- Fold?

If you answered "call," give yourself two points. This is an interesting and trapping type of play that has its merits under certain game conditions. Is it the best play here? If you play this way, you are hoping for a raise from one of the players behind you, so that you then re-raise and trap the raiser and the players between for the price of a call. Against an aggressive player who will raise small Flop bets with less than premium values, this play may make sense. Again this is a question of observing the players in your game. General game conditions as described indicate that this sort of player is not present in this game. Another response to a raise in the back may be to smooth call the raise and to come out firing on the Turn. There may be a place for this play but not here. The reason is that with this many players in the pot, in an essentially passive game, you may be giving players on draws the correct odds to call. Draws here are very likely: T9, 67, 79 (and other less probable hands) are drawing to straights and of course any player holding two hearts is drawing to a flush. If you allow players to draw and a queen or four or a heart comes on the Turn you are left in a quandary. If there is a bet and a raise you are now behind and if the action is heavy enough you may have to correctly fold your set, never a pleasant thing, or call big bets to the River with the losing hand, also distinctly unpleasant and unprofitable. Many players habitually slowplay sets on the Flop, by calling small bets on the Flop and waiting to pounce on the Turn. You must carefully choose the times to play this way, or you may play yourself out of a pot.

If you answered "raise $80–$100," give yourself five points. This is the optimal play. A raise of somewhere between two-thirds the pot or a pot-sized bet is ideal. Two-thirds the size of the pot is a tempting bet for drawing hands to call but they are making a mistake by doing so. Your raise takes away their odds. The bet from the player to your right looks like some kind of a probe bet. If instead it's designed as a trapping play you are happy to be caught because against any player except one holding a pair of jacks, you have the whip hand. If anybody with, say, top-pair or two-pair plays back at you then you can raise again. *Your objective here is to manipulate the pot so as to cause your opponents to maximize the size of their mistake.* If the player who raised to your right has any sort of hand he will play back at you and you should be willing to play a big pot with him. If he has no decent hand, then neither calling nor betting a smaller amount is going to entice him to continue, so you may as well bet an amount that you think is likely to get called and causes difficulty for your opponents, who may believe that you are raising with top-pair. *Bet when you have an advantage and bet in such a way as to maximize your opponents' errors if they play with you.* Bet too little and they can draw profitably, bet too much and they can get away from the hand error free. Correct bet size selection is a key skill and it is easy to do when you know odds and what you are attempting to achieve in the hand.

If you answered "raise all-in," give yourself one point. This is another essentially timid play although it looks at first like the opposite. Weaker players prefer not to make decisions beyond the Flop and one way of achieving that aim is to move all-in when you have a clearly strong position as you do here. Players who have recently been drawn out on will make this play a lot. The one merit of this play, and why I give you one point if you choose it, is that it is just about guaranteed to shut out drawing hands and indeed just about any other hand except maybe top set, bottom set, and possibly a player holding the ace of hearts and another heart. This play is very obviously announcing that you have a big hand and only another big hand will play against you, unless your opponents are very loose and unobservant. Remember, though, we win the most when we *play in such a way as to maximize our opponents' errors*, and this does not fit the bill.

If you answered "fold," give yourself minus five points. Okay, you win the award for Pigeon-Livered Poker Player of the Year. If you are the type of player who will only continue with the nuts as the pot gets larger you are losing money. Poker is rarely a game of certainties and you will rarely have a more favorable situation than this. You have the second best hand possible at this point and you must make hay whilst the sun shines.

Problem Eighteen: Small Pairs Can Be Hard

Theme: Getting Raised

Stack Size: Medium/Large

Position: Middle

The game is a $1-$2, $100-maximum buy-in game. There are four raises allowed per round of betting. You are new to the table and have bought-in for the maximum, $100. You have yet to play a hand but have noticed that the table has a number of tricky and aggressive players. You have decided to play fairly tight hoping to trap them if you flop a big hand. You know that pairs are good starting hands because they allow you to play for a set, an ideal trapping hand. You are in middle position just behind the Cut-Off. Two players in early position with stacks of around $100 have called and the player to your immediate right whose stack is about $120 has raised to eight dollars.

You look down to find that you hold:

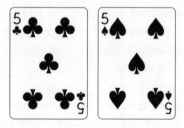

You prefer to limp for just $2 in this situation but you figure that with others calling you will probably have the odds to play on, so you call. The Cut-Off, whose stack is $60, re-raises and makes it $16 to go. The Button folds. Both Blinds fold, but the early-position limpers call the $16. When the action gets back to original raiser, who is on your right, he re-raises and makes it $35 to go. You have put in $8 and calling will cost you another $27. The pot stands at $106. Do you:

- Call?
- Raise all-in?
- Raise $70?
- Fold?

If you answered "call," give yourself one point. If you called here you made a very marginal play. There are three problems: You do not have the pot odds; the stack sizes of your opponents probably mean that you do not have the necessary implied odds; and what is worse, if you call, you cannot be certain that you will close the betting for this round. The Cut-Off may decide to raise or go all in and by that stage you are playing your small pair for a lot of money Pre-Flop. Your play no longer has positive expectation. You will not hit the Flop often enough to compensate for the times you miss it, or hit it and lose to a better hand. Remember, there is also the factor of *reverse implied odds* to consider as well. The reason I give you one point is that you may be lucky and not get raised in the back, but playing poker in the hope that things will work out is not a winning mental attitude.

If you answered "raise all-in," give yourself one point. There is little merit to this play but I give you a point for aggression. If you believe that you will go to the Flop against just the Cut-Off, whom you have covered, and the raiser to your right, who has you covered, there may be some merit in this play. However, it is likely that you are either marginally ahead or way behind, especially if you are facing an overpair. Given your hand and the action so far, this is not at all unlikely. You are only marginally ahead against high, unpaired hands and so at best you are in a race. This is entirely the wrong situation for moving all-in and you would have to believe that one or both raisers are bluffing to make this a worthwhile play.

If you answered "raise $70," give yourself minus five points. This is a pointless raise. It won't scare anybody out of the pot except players holding strong hands. If you get even one caller you are pot-committed with a hand that is looking for a big hit on the Flop. You will soon have to put in the rest of your stack and you do not yet have a favorable situation. This is not a Pre-Flop raising situation.

If you answered "fold," give yourself five points. This is the correct play. You made an error calling the original raise but there is no need to compound that error by continuing to play here. Small pairs are not meant to be played in a pot that has this much raising Pre-Flop. The strict pot odds are a just a shade worse than 4:1. If you get raised after your call, your play is essentially destroyed and it is highly likely that the re-raiser will raise here. What are you going to do when the action comes back to you? The Cut-Off has a small stack of only $60 so there is not much to win even if you hit the Flop. You are being squeezed between two raisers who are both, it appears, happy to get their money in Pre-Flop if they can, and both may be holding stronger cards than you. Continuing has negative expectation here.

Problem Nineteen: Keep Your Draws On

Theme: Playing Draws from Early Position and Reverse Implied Odds

Stack Size: Medium/Large

Position: Early

You are at a $300-maximum buy-in, $2–$5 table, and because you have been doing well you have a stack of over $450. The game conditions are ideal as the table has a number of loose but passive players, who tend to become more passive in the face of strong betting. You have loosened up your Pre-Flop calling standards a little too, and are willing to bet for value in the right circumstances.

You are under the gun and the action is on you. You look down to find:

This is the type of hand that you would prefer to play in late position, because you know it does not play well in a raised pot with few opponents. However, because the table has been so passive, you decide to take a chance and call, Pre-Flop, planning to fold if the action gets hot and heavy. The other players in early position fold, one player in middle position calls, and the Cut-Off, Button, and Big Blind limp too. The pot has five players in the hand total (including you), and the pot stands at $27. All your opponents have stacks of over $300.

The Flop is:

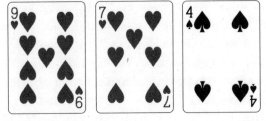

You have a flush draw and two overcards. The Big Blind checks and the action is on you.

Do you:

- Bet $5–$9?
- Bet $18–$27?
- Check and call?
- Check and raise?

If you answered "bet $5–$9," give yourself one point. This is an interesting play. It may cause the passive to fold, or entice those with weaker draws to play on so that if you make a hand on the Turn you may win a bigger pot. I see several problems with this play, however. If you open the betting and are raised behind you may play yourself out of the pot. This play is essentially a semi-bluff, but it is a pretty wimpy one if you bet a small sum like this. It is like a probe bet and may well be seen as such.

If you answered "bet $18–$27," give yourself one point. It appears you have the odds to make a strong play like this, at the pot. In the section below I question that because some outs are not outs. If you believe that leading out will let you draw a free card on the Turn this play might work. However, if you do not make your hand you have a dilemma on the Turn because if you check, it pretty much lets your opponents know that you are drawing, and if you bet, you may be raised by a player who makes a hand. You will either make your draw too pricey or play yourself out of the pot. If you do bet you may be raised by a player behind you and again you may no longer have the odds to continue to profitably draw.

If you answered "check and call," give yourself five points. The problem here is that the hand is not as good as it looks. Superficially you have a flush draw and two overcards. You have nine outs to make your flush on the Turn and three tens and three aces that appear to be outs also for a total of fifteen outs. With fifteen outs you have a 54 percent chance of making your hand either on the Turn or the River, so it appears you can bet profitably. Even if only one player calls, you would appear to have a positive expectation. However, you do not have as many outs as it seems. A ten falling may give you top-pair, but it may give another player two-pair because as in an unraised pot T9 is not an unreasonable hand for a player in late position to hold. So let's say a ten is an out and a half. Similarly an ace may not be an out either as loose-passive players routinely play hands containing an ace in an unraised pot, so with four opponents one or more could be holding hands like A9, A7, or A4. Allowing for this, let's say you have another out and a half.

Similarly, you do not really have nine outs for the flush draw since a six or eight of hearts could make a straight flush for one of your opponents. Again 65 (hearts) and even 85 (hearts) (remember the Big Blind just checked) are not impossible and are within the range of hands your opponents can hold in an unraised pot. If we then total the range of real outs that you have, it may be closer to ten to twelve and not fifteen. In fact you have a much weaker draw than it appears. If you have approximately eleven outs only when taking all this into consideration, you are roughly a 1.6:1 underdog to make your hand by either the Turn or the River. Also a four of hearts on the Turn makes you a flush but makes a player holding a set a full house. In an unraised pot any player could easily be holding pocket nines, sevens, or fours and may now be holding a set. This means that they may not only have the best hand right now but have re-draws to quads and full houses if the Board pairs on the

River and you make, say, a flush on the Turn. This is the factor of *reverse implied odds.* You must take account of these as well as implied odds when looking at draws.

In summary, in early position with a draw that has less than fourteen clean outs you are usually better calling when you have more than three opponents on the Flop.

This is a guide, not a rule, and as always game conditions must be accounted for but players often are overly optimistic about out and implied odds.

If you answered "check and raise," give yourself one point. Under certain conditions this play has merit, specifically, if you believe that some or all of your opponents will fold to a check-raise on the Flop or a continuation bet on the Turn, whether or not you make your hand. If your opponents are this passive and you have good control over them then this play can be used. This play has a number of problems, though. First, you are increasing the cost of your own draw and therefore worsening your odds. If your opponents will simply call your bets and check and call the Turn if no heart falls, or fold if it does, this play is ineffective because you have ruined your own implied odds. Second, since you are in early position, you give yourself a difficult decision on the Turn. Do you bet, if you do or do not make your card, or do you check, hoping for either a bet if you made your hand or a check from your opponents if you did not? Lastly, with this many players behind you you may find it hard to shake loose any player who has a hand or even just a straight draw. This play may give you a tricky image, but it is a high variance play that can easily backfire and be a chip drainer.

Problem Twenty: New Draws for a New Day?

Theme: Playing Draws from Late Position

Stack Size: Medium/Large

Position: Late

You are at a $300-maximum buy-in, $2–$5 table, and because you have been doing well you have a stack of over $450. The game conditions are ideal as the table has a number of loose but passive players who tend to become more passive in the face of strong betting. You have loosened up your Pre-Flop calling standards a little too, and are willing to bet for value in the right circumstances. Wait just a doggone minute! Does this problem seem familiar? Yep, just like the last one but with a significant change: You are on the Button and the action is on you. One player in early position limps, one player in middle position does likewise, and the Cut-Off limps too. The Small Blind and the Big Blind have both been pretty passive. The pot has four players in the hand total, and the pot stands at $27. All your opponents have stacks of over $300. You look down to find:

You decide to call rather than raise because you want to play the Flop and do not want to have to call a re-raise. The Small and Big Blinds both call. There are now seven players in the pot and the pot stands at $35.

The Flop is:

You are amazed to find that everyone checks the Flop and the action is on you. Do you:

- Bet $20–$30?
- Check?

If you answered "check," give yourself three points. It would be very hard to say that checking here is incorrect. See Problem Nineteen for a discussion of how many clean outs you have in this situation. You are drawing at the ace high flush, but *not* the nuts because it is possible that somebody is drawing to the *straight flush*. In an unraised pot this is much more likely. It is also harder to put people on specific hands, because most players will call with a much wider range of hands than they will raise with and especially call a raise with. Your position means that you are closing the action you are being offered unlimited odds to for your draw, so checking here is not wrong. However, I believe the more aggressive action is preferable here and below I explain why.

If you answered "bet $20–$30," give yourself five points. Many players would check here and would see no point in betting. After all, why open yourself to the possibility of a raise, which could mean that you have insufficient odds to call and see the Turn? There is a lot of merit in this argument and if the players were tricky and aggressive, this would probably be the better line of play. However, this table is passive. Nobody raised Pre-Flop and nobody bet on the Flop. It is possible that an early position player is attempting a check-raise, but it is more likely that nobody likes their hand or they are on a draw. By betting here you are playing just the same way as you would if you had hit your hand. Late-position players often will bet here in an attempt to steal the pot, so it may look like you are doing just that. If so, you will get called by those who think you are just making a move. If you bet it will be hard for your opponents to put you on a hand. If you check, they know that you are on a drawing hand. If a heart comes on the Turn, and it is checked to you, it will be hard to get anyone to call your bet on the Turn if you have checked the Flop. However, if you bet now and a heart comes, it will be hard for your opponents to know if you are bluffing or have a hand. If a heart falls on the Turn, someone may look you up to keep you honest. In this way you create the possibility of winning a bigger pot.

Also, by betting players may fold, and you are therefore increasing your pot equity. More important, aggressive action here may cause these passive players to check to you on the Turn. This gives you the option to check behind them and get yourself a *free card* on the River if the Turn does not help you.

Betting here mixes up your playing strategy, keeps your opponents guessing, and may well increase your pot equity. This line of play is not suited to all situations, but used here it increases your positive expectation and therefore your long-term win rate.

Problem Twenty-one: Overpair Aggression

Theme: Overpairs on the Flop and Beyond

Stack Size: Medium/Large

Position: Button

You are in a $500-maximum buy-in table, with Blinds of $2–$5. Your stack stands at over $750. The action is checked to a player in middle position who raises to $25. His stack covers yours and is over $1,000. The players between you fold and you look down to find that you hold:

Since you have the best Pre-Flop starting hand you decide to raise. You want some action, though, because you know that your opponent has a weaker hand so you make it $60 to go, because you believe that he may well call this amount, but not anything much larger. The Blinds fold and the action is back on the original raiser. After a short think he calls your re-raise. The pot has $127 in it and it is heads up between you and the original raiser, who you believe is a good player.

The Flop is: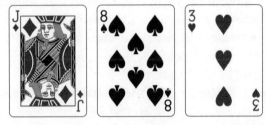

You have an overpair on the Flop and the Flop allows for little in the way of draws. To your surprise your opponent bets $60 on the Flop. The pot stands at $187. Your opponent still has over $800 in his stack. Do you:

- Call?
- Raise and make it $120 to go?
- Raise all-in?
- Raise $160–$200?

If you answered "call," give yourself one point. The bet here is a little disturbing because your Pre-Flop call more or less announced that you have a very strong hand, yet your opponent bets. If he puts you on AK and he has, say, AJ or TT then the bet makes sense. He is only betting about half the pot, so he is either probing or he wants action. Calling here really achieves nothing. If you believe you have the best hand this play is too passive. You have little reason at this stage to believe you are beaten.

If you answered "raise and make it $120 to go," give yourself three points. This bet size has pros and cons: If you are being trapped you may get away from the hand cheaply, if your opponent either raises or calls and bets the Turn. However, it also says, "I like my hand, but not a lot." Perhaps your opponent will sense weakness and try to move you off the hand now, or on the Turn, by making a big bet. This bet is better than calling but may still leave you in some doubt as to how to continue.

If you answered "raise all-in," give yourself zero points. This is lame-brained. If you have the best hand you have made it easy for your opponent to get away from the hand. If you are behind, you will lose your stack. The stacks are way too deep for this type of play to make any sense.

If you answered "raise $160–$200," give yourself five points. Your overpair is still strong. The $60 is on the low side and may only be a probing bet. A good-sized raise should settle it here. You have a strong hand, but a pair is still just a pair. If your opponent is willing to call a bet of two-thirds to a full pot-size, he is either making a big mistake or trapping. Now is the time to find out.

Problem Twenty-two: You Have to Be Watchful

Theme: Overpairs on the Flop and Beyond

Stack Size: Deep

Position: Button

The same game in Problem Twenty-One continues. You raised and made it $180 to go. Your opponent called and this troubles you. The pot stands at $487. You should be able to work out your respective stack sizes from the previous problem, but you know there is plenty left to bet.

The Turn card is:

Your opponent bets $200. Do you:

- Call?
- Raise?
- Move all-in?
- Fold?

If you answered "call," give yourself zero points. In limit poker, calling to the River may make sense in a similar situation where you hold a big overpair and the pot is large in relation to the size of potential calls. In no-limit play, calling here results in needless losses. If your opponent bets half the pot on the River and you do not make a set on the River, what will you do?

If you answered "raise," give yourself minus five points. Raising has not shaken this player loose on the Flop and will not here, if he has any sort of hand. Does he? He can no longer have AJ, as he would not have been willing to call your raise on the Flop and bet the Turn when a queen falls. QJ makes some sense but he was willing to take a lot of heat before making two-pair on the Turn so it seems somewhat unlikely that this is his hand. It looks like he either called with JJ Pre-Flop and made a set or was willing to continue with QQ on the Flop and has made a set now. Of course, he could also have KK and you may be ahead, but his willingness to continue calling raises and betting out makes it doubtful that he has only one pair, even pocket kings. If he does, this is the only credible hand you are beating. It seems foolish to put him on this hand and only this hand as a reason for continuing. *Remember, you must put opponents on a range of hands.*

If you answered "move all-in," give yourself minus ten points. With shallow stacks this might make some sense. Here it is just an invitation to get stacked. You will only get called by a better hand. You are risking a lot to make (comparatively) a little. This is misplaced aggression. You had a big hand Pre-Flop, but now you only have one pair. Given the action and your opponent's play, you are no longer willing to play a big pot.

If you answered "fold," give yourself five points. You made a decent-size raise, got called, and your opponent comes out betting. The Q could easily have made him two-pair or a set of queens. Two-pair is unlikely given the Pre-Flop and Flop action. A pair of ladies fits with all his previous actions: a raise Pre-Flop, an overpair on the Flop, and now a set. The other possibility is that he made a set on the Flop. It is unlikely he would have raised and called a re-raise Pre-Flop with a pair of eights or threes, but a pair of jacks again fits logically with all of his actions Pre-Flop and beyond. Your actions tell him that you are likely to have aces or kings and he seems unfazed by the queen on the Turn. This bet looks like he wants you to call. One pair is not enough to continue here against a player with a deep stack. You may only have two outs.

Problem Twenty-three: Fighting Fire

Theme: Blocking Bets

Stack Size: Deep

Position: Cut-Off

The game is a $500-maximum buy-in, $2–$5 game with a number of aggressive opponents who like to raise the pot Pre-Flop. Their presence means that you have tightened up your opening hand selection. However you noticed that these same players will rarely re-raise. Your stack is over $1200 and so are the stacks of a number of other players.

The action has been passive this hand. There are three limpers, one in early position and two in middle position. You look down to find you hold:

The players in the pot have fairly deep stacks and the stacks of both Blinds are at least as large as yours. However the player on the Button and the players in the Blinds are aggressive and like to make big Pre-Flop raises, even out of position. Do you:

- Call?
- Raise to $30?
- Raise to $15?
- Fold?

If you answered "call," give yourself one point. This problem presents some difficult choices and the playability of any option depends upon the specific game conditions. It also shows how the presence of two or three aggressive players makes the game much more difficult to play well and almost certainly adds to your variance. Calling here is not wrong, as you are hoping to limp with a drawing hand, but with three aggressive players yet to act, and one who will have position on you in future betting rounds, it is unlikely to do well. If the players yet to act raise four to five times the Big Blind, you will probably have to fold, unless the other limpers all call too. You want to play your hand against multiple opponents. Calling is usually the solution but ironically it may be counterproductive here.

If you answered "raise to $30," give yourself one point. This raise is the right idea, but the wrong amount. Your objective is to bet in such a way that you make it attractive for others with large stacks to call. If you are re-raised when making this bet you probably should fold, and you have made the play costly for yourself. If this raise causes you to be in a pot with, for example, one other player who is willing to call your raise, it is likely that you are against a better hand. If you Flop an ace you may well be behind.

If you answered "raise to $15," give yourself five points. Raising here so that you can profitably play a drawing hand seems counter-intuitive at first. To make this play you must be aware of game conditions. Specifically the aggressive players seem to like to build pots Pre-Flop, but only if they can initiate the action. This bet essentially sets the bet size for future action. It is a kind of Pre-Flop blocking bet. You make this bet to avoid having to call a raise that is really too large to be optimal. The players behind you like to raise but not re-raise. Your raise here may buy you the Button, or cause the players behind, including the Button and the limpers, to call too. The downside of course is that the players behind may re-raise if they perceive your raise as weakness. If they are unsure, though, they will probably only call your small raise, and this is the point of the play. This is one reason why you must sometimes make small raises with big hands as well as mediocre hands like this one. It keeps your opponents guessing and means they cannot easily put you on a hand when you make a small raise.

If you are re-raised heavily you can fold when the action gets back to you, but you have put yourself in a position to win a big pot if there are no re-raises and the Flop is favorable. You want the Flop to be kind, and you should be reluctant to continue if the Flop does not hit you, or at least give you a big draw, which is the most likely *favorable* Flop that you will get. What also makes this small raise the best choice is the large stack size of your opponents that give you good implied odds. If you or your opponents had small stacks this would not be the optimal play.

If you answered "fold," give yourself two points. Folding here cannot be heavily criticized because you have a mediocre starting hand and aggressive players yet to act. However, you may be giving up too much in a game like this, if you are only willing to play premium hands. You may get little action, because when you do enter a pot players will be unwilling to play against you. Against observant opponents in live games, you have to mix up your play a little if you wish to maintain positive expectation overall.

Problem Twenty-four: Calling for Value

Theme: Implied Odds and Draws

Stack Size: Deep

Position: Button

The game is a $500-maximum buy-in, $2–$5 game. Your stack is over $1,000. Around the table the stacks vary considerably in size but a number of players also have fairly deep stacks. Pre-Flop you called with:

That was because there were three limpers and the game was reasonably passive. The Blinds limped too and therefore there were six players in an unraised pot before the Flop. The pot contained $30. The Flop barely hit you, as it is what's shown at the top of the next page:

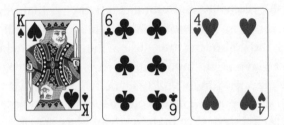

However, it was checked to you and in an attempt to steal the pot you bet $20. Two players called and the pot stands at $90 and both your opponents have big stacks. The Turn is another low card but one that helps you. It is:

One player checked but the other bet $30. The action is on you. Do you:

- Raise?
- Call?
- Fold?

If you answered "raise," give yourself one point. Raising may win you the pot right here, but it is not best. You may get re-raised but worse than that, you lose the chance of winning a potentially bigger pot. Your hand is well disguised and you have many outs. If you make your hand on the River you can bet or raise with a high likelihood of at least one caller. If not, your position on the Button allows you to check the River down or fold to a bet. Here the more passive play has the greater positive expectation.

If you answered "call," give yourself five points. There are two factors that make this the optimal play. One is that your hand is well disguised and this means that your implied odds are better than, say, if the Board had three hearts and you only held the ace of hearts. Implied odds are not just about your opponents' stack sizes but also about the likelihood of making more money if you hit your hand. You probably have fifteen clean outs here going to the River. You are drawing to the ace high flush, and any ace or seven probably wins you the pot. If your opponents have a weak king, the ace falling on the River will probably not elicit a call, but a seven will. If either opponent is drawing to a heart flush, you will get paid off on the River. Even if they are not, it is hard to put you on a flush draw, and so you are likely to get your bet called if another heart falls, because your bet may be interpreted as merely a pot-stealing attempt.

If you answered "fold," give yourself one point. You have not risked much on this hand and may be behind so folding is not a complete error with one card to come. However, if you fold like this for a bet the size of the pot too frequently, it will be easy for anyone to bet you out of a pot. If you play this tightly, then when you make your hand you will get no action and you will effectively lose your implied odds. A hand this well disguised is certainly worth a call. Also, if the other player calls too you have an even better chance of getting paid off on the River if your hand improves.

Problem Twenty-five: Best Hand, Poor Position

Theme: Out of Position with Deep Stacks

Stack Size: Deep

Position: Big Blind

The game is a $500-maximum buy-in, $2–$5 game and the stacks are mixed. There is at least one aggressive good player to your right and now on the Button, who has a big stack. The other players are of mixed abilities and have small and medium-sized stacks. One player has limped into the pot from middle position and the aggressive player on the Button seems to sense weakness and has raised to $15. You sense that he is using his stack size, position, and image to intimidate the other players and in this instance is raising to drive out the Blinds, but perhaps with a less-than-premium hand.

You look down to find that you have:

Not too bad a hand and one where with the right Flop you may be able to make some money from the Button. You call the raise and so does the other player left in the hand. The pot is three-way, with both players having position on you. There is $47 in the pot.

The Flop comes down:

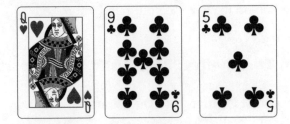

Not exactly the Flop you had hoped for, as you have no straight or flush draw, but you do have top pair with a good kicker. You decide to take the aggressive course and bet $35. The player in middle position quickly folds but the Button, who is tough, raises and makes it $100 to go. His stack size indicates that he has at least $1,200 left to bet and your stack stands at a little over $600. Do you:

- Call?
- Re-raise?
- Fold?

If you answered "call," give yourself zero points. If you call what do you do on the Turn and River? If your opponent is holding a flush draw and A9 or A5 and a flush card or an ace fall, you have a tough decision. He can bet for value and you can do little. It gets worse, however: If the cards fall and he bets but does *not* have the hand he is representing, how can you tell? His aggressive playing style and his betting pattern combine here to give you little certain information. Calling leaves you vulnerable and in a mysterious position.

If you answered "re-raise," give yourself minus five points. This play makes little sense here. Even if you have the best hand you have problems on the Turn and River, because your opponent's position means he can get away from the hand cheaply and easily. By contrast, if you do not have the best hand, or his hand improves, and you continue, you stand to lose a big pot. It seems that you can only win a small pot or lose a large one if you raise, neither of which are good options.

If you answered "fold," give yourself five points. If you are a limit player, folding top pair with a good kicker might seem like heresy, but this is *not* limit poker. Ironically, having the best hand is only part of the equation here and you cannot be certain you even have that. Even with the best hand your options on the Turn and River are poor. If you call down bets because you believe your opponent is bluffing or semi-bluffing, and the Button has the goods, you have allowed him to make bets for value. If he bets as a bluff how could you tell he is bluffing? If you fold to a Turn or River bet he is using his stack and image to push you off the best hand. Again, there is little you can do about it, though. A pair is only a pair, and if you decide to go to war with it you could end up losing a good portion of your stack if you are beaten. In this case the

Button is in charge and can easily manipulate the pot, ensuring that you make a big mistake as you play on. You have taken a shot at the pot and you got resistance. Time to move on.

This problem illustrates how hard it is to play out of position, against a decent player who has a deep stack. It also demonstrates that you must consider not only whether or not you have the best hand, but factors such as position, stack size, and player type when playing no-limit Hold'em. Deeper stacks often mean more complex decisions and that is one reason why you must be careful about when you get involved. It is not just about who has the best hand.

Problem Twenty-six: Slowplaying Has Its Place

Theme: Slowplaying Big Hands

Stack Size: Deep

Position: Big Blind

The game is a $500-maximum buy-in, $2–$5 game. The stacks around the table are medium to deep. Game conditions are mixed with some passive and some aggressive players. You pick up:

One early- and one middle-position player have limped and the Button, usually a more aggressive player, has limped too. The Small Blind, a rock, folds and you are happy to check your option. Four players, including you, see the Flop.

The Flop is:

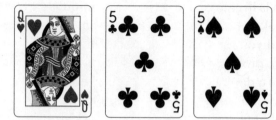

There is $27 in the pot and you check, hoping another player will bet. To your disappointment it is checked to the Button, who bets $15. The action is on you and the pot contains $42. Do you:

- Raise?
- Call?

If you answered "raise," give yourself zero points. The pot here is small and you want action. You probably have the best hand. At this stage you do not want to discourage any player holding a queen.

If you answered "call," give yourself five points. The bet by the Button has very little meaning. On a Board like this, when a player bets first he often wins the pot. This bet will be seen as what it is by most players, and that is an attempt to pick up this small pot quickly and cheaply. Your hand is too strong and the pot too small to raise yet, especially since players behind you may have a hand they want to continue with. Call and see what happens, as your hand can stand a lot of heat and if players behind are overly aggressive, you may win a decent pot.

The other players are unconvinced by the Button's bet and both call. The pot is $87. The Turn card is shown on the next page:

Do you:

- Bet half the pot?
- Check?

If you answered "bet half the pot," give yourself two points. This play might make sense if you believe that a player behind you will call or put in a small raise, and the Button might do just that. However this looks like a classic slowplay from early position and if one of your opponents has something, but not much, it is likely to induce a fold. You still have a very strong hand and want to see the pot grow.

If you answered "check," give yourself five points. The jack on the Turn is a good card for you. If you are lucky it will make someone two-pair as many players will play QJ in an unraised pot. If it does, then that player will have a hard job getting away from the hand and unless another queen or jack falls on the River you will do well. Again, you want to encourage players who have second-best hands to continue and players holding hands like KQ and KJ may still stick around as it looks like they have the best hand. The Button's bet shook nobody loose. This could be because nobody believed him but it could also be because somebody has a hand they like and is also slowplaying! If they have a hand like 56 you are in good shape. The only problem is if another player is holding A5 suited, a much more likely hand in an unraised pot in no-limit. If so, you stand to lose a big pot and there is little you can do. *The ideal slowplay candidate is a hand that is close to the nuts but not in fact the* *nuts.* Your hand here fits the bill well. Checking here is the preferred play because it gives those behind a chance to catch up, reveals nothing about your hand strength, may trap players for more chips, builds a larger pot, may induce a bluff from the Button, and protects you if you are behind to a hand like A5. Wow! The wonders of a check in the right place.

If somebody does take a stab at the pot here, you could call again, bet out on the River, or raise here on the Turn. If the players were more aggressive you may even just smooth call any bet on the Turn. You have many options here, but right now checking is the strongest play. If you had only one opponent, however, then betting would be a better option, unless your one opponent was very aggressive. Checking here works, because there is a good chance of a bet from a player behind you and the pot is still small in relation to the other players' stacks. Players making second-best hands to your best hands are where you make your money in poker.

Problem Twenty-seven: To Slowplay or Not?

Theme: Playing with the Nuts

Stack Size: Deep

Position: Middle

The game is a $500-maximum buy-in, $2–$5 game. A number of players are aggressive and tough and the stacks are deep. A player in early position limps and another immediately to your right raises to $20.

You hold:

Since you know that jacks play badly against multiple opponents you raise and make it $60 to go. The Button, an aggressive
player, calls; the limper in early position folds; and the original
raiser, a fairly tough and aggressive player, calls too. The pot stands
at $192.

The Flop is:

Of course the other way JJ make money is when they flop a set or
better in a multi-opponent pot! If only you knew that the Flop was
going to be like this, you would have encouraged callers! Hold'em
would be so much easier if we could play backward. You have
flopped the nuts, and the question is how to make the most money
from it. Your chances of being outdrawn here are minuscule, so
how to maximize the advantage?

To your surprise the player to your right checks. The action is on
you. Do you:

- Bet $125?
- Bet $200–$300?
- Check?

If you answered "bet $125," give yourself five points. This is the right move and the right amount. If your opponents are used to seeing you regularly make bets of two-thirds to one full pot size on the Flop, it will be hard for them to know how strong your hand is. You could argue that any bet may chase them out of the pot, and this is true if either they are passive players or have no hand at all. In this case, however, you are playing against two aggressive players who are unlikely to be chased out of a pot by a bet of this size. Let's consider what hands they might have: It is easily possible that either or both of them have an overpair such as queens, kings, or aces. It is also possible that they hold AK, or even AQ (AJ and AT and even KQ are also possibilities, but are much less likely given the nature of the Pre-Flop action). If either of them holds an overpair, then you're going to get action on the Flop and beyond. Of course, if they do, there is a danger that an ace, king, or queen will fall on the Turn or River and you will lose the pot. This is a risk that you have to take because the range of hands with which you may get callers and that you can beat, if they get no help on subsequent streets, is far greater than the number of hands that could beat you. Quite simply, you have the best of it right now; your hand is extremely strong and can barely improve and so you must bet and hope that your opponents have a good, but inferior, hand with which to call. If they have no hand with which they are willing to continue, then it doesn't matter what you would bet, because they would fold to any bet regardless of size. Your ideal situation, of course, is if somebody is slowplaying a hand like A5 (suited), because you are almost certain to stack them or double through if they cover you. *The rule here is to be less inclined to slowplay the nuts, because doing so may cost you a lot in positive expectation.*

If you answered "bet $200–$300," give yourself 2 points. This is the right idea but this bet is too large. You want to attract callers, not chase them out of the pot. Some opponents regard an oversize bet as a sign that you hold only a mediocre hand and therefore will raise or go all-in. If this were to happen, you would, of course, be happy to play this hand for all your chips, as you are an over-whelming favorite in almost all circumstances. Of course, unless your opponents are hyper-aggressive or view you as a very weak player, this is not likely to happen. In fact, with stacks as deep as this, the most likely result is that both players will fold. Conse-quently, you really haven't maximized your expectation.

If you answered "check," give yourself zero points. How can it be an error to slowplay the nuts when it is correct to slowplay an in-ferior hand that is close to the nuts? Many players automatically slowplay the nuts, especially when they Flop a monster hand such as the one above. On the very rare occasions that you flop quads, slowplaying makes sense, because you have crippled the deck and there are very few second-best hands that players can make. You are hoping that they make something on the Turn or on the River and therefore will bet or call bets. This situation is quite different. Here, there is a potential for many second-best hands and aggres-sive and tough players are unlikely to be intimidated by a bet on the Flop. In fact, it could be argued that to check and then bet the Turn is more likely to arouse suspicion in a tough player. By check-ing, you may cost yourself a lot of chips. Another, though less im-portant, consideration is that your opponents' overpairs give them redraws to your full house. If you give them unlimited odds to draw at the turn, and they spike a card that makes them a higher full house, you are going to make playing decisions for yourself ex-tremely difficult on the Turn and the River. An ace, king, or queen on the Turn may make your opponent a higher full house, but it could also make him only top-pair if he holds, say, AK or AQ. Checking is a poor play in this situation, and is no way to maximize your positive expectation.

Problem Twenty-eight: Big Hands, Loose Players

Theme: Pre-Flop Loose Opponents

Stack Size: Medium

Position: Middle

The game is a $500-maximum buy-in, $2–$5 game. You have a stack of $600. To your left and on the Button sits a player who is loose and aggressive. Specifically he plays too many hands Pre-Flop, and is willing to commit his stack with them. He seems to like to try to dominate the table, push players off hands, and intimidate them. You believe that he views you as a weak player. His stack is a little over $800.

There has been a call to your right from a fairly loose but more passive player. You look down and find you hold:

You raise to $35. The Button re-raises to $120. There is $167 in the pot because when the action gets back to you, both Blinds and the early position limper have folded. You have $565 left to bet and the action is on you. Do you:

- Fold?
- Call?
- Re-raise to $300?
- Move all-in?

If you answered "fold," give yourself minus five points. This is way too tight. The only player that folding may be justified against is a rock who will only re-raise with a very narrow range of hands. In all other cases you have a premium hand and an opportunity to get your money in when you almost certainly have the best of it. This is what you should do here. You cannot play only AA or KK when facing a re-raise, especially against a player who is habitually too loose Pre-Flop.

If you answered "call," give yourself one point. There is some but not much merit in this play. On the plus side, if you have an overpair when the Flop comes or flop a set, you may be able to move in then and get a call. Another plus is that you are going to play the pot heads up and this is best for jacks. You can also play jacks for a call in a multi-way pot where you figure to make money by flopping a set. A call here is too passive, though, and keeps the positional advantage with the Button. If you move all-in, the Button's positional advantage disappears. The key point is that you are almost certainly leading right now and you are passing up an opportunity to get your money in when you have the lead.

If you answered "re-raise to $300," give yourself two points. This is the right idea, but the wrong amount. By making this call you have committed over half of your stack to the pot. A loose and aggressive player like this is likely to call you with an inferior hand. Give him the opportunity to make as large a mistake as possible.

If you answered "move all-in," give yourself five points. This is the correct move here. The re-raise from the Button may be an attempt to bully you. You have the fourth best hand in Hold'em and one that, ideally, you want to play heads up. If you believe that this player in this position will call with inferior hands such as AQ, AJ, or even AT and, say, middle pairs, you have the odds clearly in your favor. Even against a better hand such as AK you are still the favorite. Of course, if he has AA–QQ you are in trouble but even then you still have outs. Remember, the essence of winning no-limit Hold'em is to play so that you attract calls from inferior hands. You should also be inclined to move in because the player on the Button views you as weak and he likes to intimidate players. This type of player will often call because he resents a player who plays back at him. Make him pay. This type of situation in a loose game may account for a major part of your winnings.

Problem Twenty-nine: Top Pair, No Good

Theme: Hands That Have Little Development Potential Post-Flop

Stack Size: Medium

Position: Big Blind

The game is a $500-maximum buy-in, $2–$5 game and somewhat passive. As the game has been going for less than an hour, no player has a stack larger than $700. Your stack is $550. There are four callers plus the Small Blind, who completes his bet before the action gets to you. Your hand is:

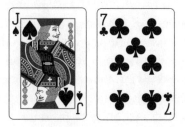

Naturally you check. The pot is six handed and there is $30 in it.

The Flop is:

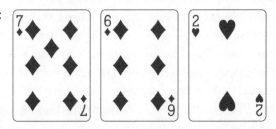

You have top-pair. The Small Blind bets $30. There are four play-ers to act after you. Do you:

- Fold?
- Call?
- Raise to $60 to $90?

If you answered "fold," give yourself five points. Top-pair is not always playable in no-limit. Here you have many players be-hind you and you have a hand that has no flush or straight poten-tial. You are out of position and your hand may not even be leading now as 67 and A7 are not at all unlikely in a passive game where no player has raised Pre-Flop. Playing on will make your playing deci-sions very difficult and thus greatly increase the chance of error. You have played this hand only because you had the option of checking in the Big Blind. Getting married to top-pair here with hands that could be beating you now and with other hands that have drawing potential is a mistake. Fold and wait for a better opportunity.

If you answered "call," give yourself zero points. Even top-pair makes a poor call here. Your only chance of improvement is for one of the two sevens or one of the three jacks to fall. You may not have the best hand now and the sevens may not be an out so you may have only three clean outs. Your call may also encourage players behind you who are drawing to flushes and straights to call too, as they may well be getting the pot odds and probably the implied odds to do so once the action gets to them. So you end up in a multi-way pot with a hand that may not be leading and that has lit-tle chance of improvement. This is a poor play.

If you answered "raise," give yourself minus five points. You cannot control other players with a hand like this from early posi-tion. If the Small Blind is willing to bet the Flop with so many play-ers behind, you must figure he has something unless he is a very weak player. Even if you figure you have him beaten a raise is still a poor play. Even if the players behind you fold, what will you do if the Small Blind re-raises when the action gets back to you? You do not have a hand that you want to play a big pot with and if you fold to a re-raise or a bet on the Turn you have wasted $60 to $90 depending on the size of the raise.

Problem Thirty: To Bet or Not to Bet?

Theme: Check-Raising Post-Flop

Stack Size: Medium

Position: Middle

The game is a $500-maximum buy-in, $2–$5 game and somewhat passive. No player has a stack larger than $700. Your stack is $600. Your hand is:

This is not your favorite hand but the table has been fairly passive and when the action gets to you there have been no bets. You decide to just limp. The players behind you fold except for the Button whom you have identified as a decent player but one who seems to make a lot of standard, rather unimaginative plays. His stack is about $700 too. He often bets half the pot on the Flop and you have seen him make a lot of continuation bets when he has position. He puts in a raise, surprise, surprise, and makes it $20 to go. The Blinds fold and the action is back on you. Since you have played with the Button before and know that he raises limpers from this position with almost anything, you decide to call. The pot contains $47 and is being contested heads up.

The Flop is:

The action is on you. Do you:

- Bet?
- Check and raise?
- Check and call?
- Check and fold to a bet?

If you answered "bet," give yourself two points. At least you are showing some aggression and taking the initiative. However, your opponent has position on you and what are you going to do if he raises? The most likely result is that you will lose your bet if he raises. If he just smooth calls, you create a problem for yourself on the Turn; do you bet or check? Is he trapping or not? If your opponent is very passive this could be the correct play with a ragged Board like this, but here there is a stronger play.

If you answered "check and raise," give yourself five points. This is the strongest play here and a fairly standard check-raising opportunity that occurs frequently in no-limit Hold'em. Here this play is best because you know that your opponent habitually makes continuation bets with nothing or very little. You are punishing his unimaginative and obvious plays. Remember, most Flops hit nobody most of the time. In a heads-up pot like this where your opponent is playing the Button, there is a good chance that he entered with weak cards and has flopped nothing. When you check-raise him you force him to make very difficult decisions where any play he makes except a re-raise, if he believes you are only making a move, is likely to be an error. He has to be very certain you have nothing to make a re-raise. What does the pot look like from *his* viewpoint? Well, he made a book-standard series of plays: raise a limper from the Button and make a continuation bet on the Flop when you check, showing what he believed was weakness. Now your check-raise has forced him to change his view. Normally in no-limit Hold'em a check-raise indicates a very strong hand. Unless he has a monster or a very good read on you, how can he continue? The Board is ragged and you limped, but had a strong-enough hand to call his Pre-Flop raise. Have you flopped a straight with 9T? Perhaps, he thinks, you are slowplaying a set? Two-pair is not out of the question either. From *your* standpoint you have little except an inside straight draw, overcards, and a back-door flush. What you do have is a good read on how your opponent plays.

This play does of course have risks. If your opponent really does have something he may re-raise. If he does that, you can of course abandon the pot. If he is very good he may pick up that you are bluffing (if you want to include your drawing possibilities we can flatter ourselves that this is a semi-bluff but those possibilities are a little too remote for that) and raise you back. However, he is not a very imaginative player and if he thinks you are like him he will merely believe that you are slowplaying a monster. If he calls, you have a decision to make on the Turn. My tendency would be to bet half the pot on the Turn. If firing the second bullet does not cause him to fold, check the River and fold to a bet unless you make a decent hand, because you have nothing and he likes his hand enough to continue. Also, this is not a play to make in a multi-opponent pot, because then it is much more likely that another player has enough to continue. Your check-raise heads up is a strong play because the specific situation and your knowledge of your opponent's play combine to create circumstances in which you are likely to steal the pot.

Incidentally, if the Button checks behind you he gives you a free card, and depending upon the Turn card you can elect to bet or check. My tendency would be to bet the Turn in almost all circumstances.

If you answered "check and call," give yourself zero points. This is a very weak play. You have overcards and an inside straight draw but you are really just behaving as a calling station. You are hoping to make something on the Turn but you really do not have the correct odds for a call and your play is too passive. In a heads-up pot in no-limit poker this type of play will lose you a lot of money over time. You cannot just call raises Pre-Flop and give up every time you make nothing on the Flop in a heads-up pot.

If you answered "check and fold to a bet," give yourself one point. Again a passive play and not entirely wrong since you have little on the Flop. However, if you intended to play like this, then calling the raise Pre-Flop was a mistake: You should have just folded when the Button raised. You are really playing in a fashion more suited to a multi-way pot, where you perhaps limp in and hope to flop big. This is the opposite situation. You called a raise out of position and are playing a heads-up pot against a player whose play you have observed. You are now playing the man, not just your cards. You must play the Flop and beyond with more imagination than this if you want to beat more than just the easiest games.

CHAPTER SEVEN

Conclusion and Your Quiz Scores

Did you read the problems and try to figure out the answers? I hope so. I have by no means covered all no-limit Hold'em situations. What I have aimed to achieve is to set you on a path of correct thinking. If you grasp the essential concepts you will be able to analyze the situations you encounter at the tables with greater certainty.

The Scores

If you scored 120 to 150 points you are a very strong player, or you cheated! You should do well in all but the toughest games and I would rather not play with you.

If you scored 90 to 119 points your play is reasonable but lacks imagination and you have a number of major weaknesses. You will do well in games with loose and passive players, but you need to improve your skills to succeed in tougher games.

If you scored 30 to 89 points you have a number of major weaknesses in your game and thinking. You will have some good sessions but you are probably losing long-term. You need to work hard to improve your game.

If you scored under 30 points (or even made a negative score) please tell me where you play because I will follow you around to get in a game with you. You are either a very new player, and should read a more basic book; have watched too much TV poker; or live in an aquarium. Do not enter any but the smallest games until you have learned a lot more about no-limit Hold'em.

Work through these problems again and try to construct some of your own. Review your hands away from the table and seek to constantly improve your decision-making. Remember, though, poker is still only a game. Enjoy it but don't make it the only thing in your life. Creation has more wonders than green felt, a stack of chips, and a deck of cards. If you meet a funny-looking English guy at the tables, say hello. It could be me!

Glossary

In this glossary, you will find most every term you will run across in a Hold'em game. I have also expanded on some of these on my Web site, www.holdempokernow.com. Check it out, as you will also find supplementary articles and links on poker and gaming.

AA (Two Aces)   Many poker hands have nicknames. This is the best Pre-Flop hand you can have in Hold'em. It is sometimes called "American Airlines," "Pocket Rockets," or "Bullets."

Action (the Action)   This is the betting in a specific hand or game. If the dealer says, "The action is on you," it means that it is your turn to act. A game with a lot of betting and raising is said to have lots of action.

Active Player   Any player still in the pot.

Add-On   In poker tournaments, there is often one final opportunity to re-buy a specific number of tournament chips. This is the add-on.

Advertise   Showing down a mediocre hand with the deliberate intention of posing as a weak-loose player and to establish an image, perhaps false, as such.

Aggressive   A style of play where the player bets, raises, and re-raises a lot. Some people think all good players are aggressive. Not so. They are *selectively* aggressive.

All-In   When a player has all of his chips in the pot, he is said to be all-in. In table stakes games, this can only be the amount of money you actually have on the table at the start of the hand. Once a player is all-in, he cannot call additional bets or raises. Any additional bets go into a separate side pot in which the all-in player has no stake.

Angle   A legal but ethically dubious practice. (This definition may apply to the vast majority of U.S. lawyers, come to think of it.) For example, if you pretend to go to your chips out of turn to discourage a player from betting.

Ante   Found in some poker games such as Seven-Card Stud or Draw Poker. This is a small forced bet at the beginning of each round of play that every player has to put in the pot. The purpose is to encourage people to play and not just wait for the best hand, which would be the best play if no ante was required. There is no ante in Hold'em but two forced bets called the "Big Blind" and the "Small Blind," in which every player has two put in the pot when he is one or two to the left of the dealer button.

Backdoor   Catching the Turn and River card to make a drawing hand. A "backdoor flush draw" is made when you hold only one card of the suit that you need and it appears on the Flop. If two more of the same suit come on the Turn and River, you have made a backdoor flush, also known as making a runner-runner hand.

Bad Beat   If a player holds a hand that is a heavy favorite to win and a hand that is a heavy underdog beats it, the losing player is said to have taken a bad beat. If you sit around a poker table long enough, some players are likely to regale you with stories of the bad beats they have taken. Everybody takes bad beats, and the better you play the more you are going to take. Hearing about them becomes tedious. If I suspect a fellow player is about to start whining about a bad beat, I stop him and tell him that I charge $5 to listen to a bad beat story. This usually ensures that you do not become a bad beat misery aunt at the table!

Bad Beat Jackpot See *Jackpot*.

Bad Game A game in which your opponents outclass you and are too good for you to expect a win. You should avoid games in which you are the underdog, as you will invariably lose your money to better players.

Bankroll The total amount of money you have available to wager. This is usually and should be substantially more than you bring to the table for an individual session of play.

Belly Buster An inside straight draw. When you hit a belly buster, it means you drew the card to make your inside straight. A "double belly buster" is a hand that is composed of two in-side straight draws, giving you the same odds as an open-ended straight draw.

Best of It A situation in which a wager can be expected to be profitable over time. In a table game such as roulette, the casino or house is said to always have the best of it because the odds are always in favor of the house.

Bet (or **Bet Out)** To put money into the pot that other players must match to remain in the hand.

Bet for Value To bet in order to be called by an inferior hand. You are betting in the hope that your opponents will call but not fold, so you can make more money.

Betting Round The series of checks, bets, or raises made in turn by all eligible players before more cards are dealt or there is a showdown. In Hold'em, there is a maximum of four betting rounds in each hand.

Bettor The player who first puts chips in the pot in any given round.

Big Blind   The larger of the two blinds in a Hold'em game. The Big Blind is usually a sum equal to the full first round bet, although in some pot-limit and no-limit games it may be less. The Big Blind is the player two seats to the left of the dealer button. Each player becomes Big Blind in turn as the dealer button moves clockwise around the table.

Big Slick   Slang for ace and king, before the Flop.

Blank   A card that is of no apparent value to any player's hand and does not affect the standing of the players in the pot.

Blind   The forced bets that players must make to begin a betting round. In most limit Hold'em games there are two blinds: the Big Blind and the Small Blind. The Big Blind is usually one full bet, and the Small Blind half or occasionally one-third or two-thirds of the Big Blind. The player whose turn it is to put up this bet is said to be "in the Blind."

Bluff   To bet or raise with a hand that you do not believe to be the best hand and has little or no chance of becoming so, even when there are more cards to come. This is a pure bluff. You can only win if all the other players remaining in the pot fold. You should bluff infrequently in low-limit games and just about never against a very poor player. Very poor players will tend to call, making bluffing an unprofitable play against them.

Board   All the community cards in a Hold'em game are said to make up the board. They are placed face up in the middle of the table and any player can use these cards to make up his hand.

Boat   Slang for a full house.

Bottom Pair   Pairing the lowest card on the board.

Broadway   An ace-high straight.

Brush   The casino staff member responsible for seating players in a game. He "brushes them in." He ensures that games are filled in an orderly fashion and maintains a waiting list if the games are full.

Burn (or **Burn Card)**   To burn a card means to discard the top card from the deck face down. The dealer will burn a card before each betting round and before he puts down the next community card on the board. The purpose is to provide a security measure to prevent players from gaining an advantage by catching a glimpse of the next card.

Bust   To lose all of one's playing stake.

Busted Hand   A hand that does not develop into anything of value. A flush draw that never actually becomes a flush is said to be a "busted flush."

Button   A white disk placed in front of a player that indicates he is the nominal dealer. The player "on the Button" is the last player to act in each betting round except the first. The live player closest to the Button will act last in each betting round. For example, when another player says "the Button re-raised," he means the player on the Button re-raised.

Buy ("...the Pot" or **"...Button")**   To "buy the pot" is to bluff hoping to win the pot when nobody calls. A player is said to "buy the Button" when he is not on the Button but bets or raises hoping to make other players between him and the Button fold and thus ensuring that he is last to act on each subsequent betting round.

Buy-In   The minimum stake required to sit in a particular game.

Call   To put into the pot a sum of money equal to the last bet or raise.

Call a Raise Cold   To call a double bet, that is, a bet and a raise.

Caller   Player who calls

Calling Station   A passive player who calls a lot but rarely bets or raises. Many players like this usually make for a profitable, low-risk game.

Cap   To put in the last permitted raise in a betting round. The player who does this is said to have "capped the pot." When a player says "cap it," he is announcing that he is making the last permitted raise in that round of betting. Most card rooms allow a maximum of three raises in each betting round. If there are only two players contesting a pot, it is said to be heads up, and then an unlimited number of raises are usually allowed. Some players like to say "cappuccino"—very yuppie.

Cards Speak Rule   This means the best hand at the showdown will win the pot. You do not need to declare your hand. The dealer will let the cards speak and give the pot to the player with the best hand.

Case   The last card of a specific rank in the deck is said to be the case card.

Center Pot   Alternative name for the main pot that is formed in the center of the table as the dealer collects chips from each betting round.

Chase   When a player continues in a hand (with a draw) with a hand that he knows is inferior to his opponent's hand, he is said to be chasing. In low-limit games, players often chase with very poor hands.

Check   To not bet with the option to call or raise later in the betting round. If everybody checks, then the next betting round is started.

Check-raise   To check and then raise after an opponent bets. Some players maintain that check-raising is unethical. Utter hogwash. It is a vital tactic in limit Hold'em, and you should never play in a card room that does not allow it. Without it, the players on the Button and in late position have an enormous edge.

Chips   The tokens used in place of money in a game. Some people also call these "checks." Also, the snacks brought to you (in the United States at least) by seductive waitstaff during a game.

Cinch   The best possible hand given the board when all the cards are out. Also called "the nuts."

Come Hand   A drawing hand.

Community Cards   The cards dealt face up in the center of the board that active players use to form their hands. Hold'em is described as a community card style of poker.

Complete Hand   A hand that is defined by all five cards. It can be a straight, flush, full house, four of a kind, or a straight flush.

Connector   A starting hand in Hold'em in which the two cards are one rank apart, for example, 8,9 or Q,J. Suited connectors are when both cards are of the same suit.

Counterfeit   To pretend to be a good player; not really, that was a bad joke. When a board card duplicates one of your pocket cards and makes your hand less valuable, you have been "counterfeited." For example, if you hold 8,10 and the board is 7,9,J on the Flop, and a T comes on the Turn, your hand now has just about no value. The T counterfeited you.

Crack   When a hand, usually a big hand such as pocket aces or kings, gets beaten, it is said to be cracked.

Cripple the Deck   This means that you hold most or all the cards that somebody would want to have to make their hand. When you flop four of a kind, you cripple the deck. When you cripple the deck, you will probably win your hand, but you may not get much action.

Crying Call   A call with a hand, usually at the end, that you think has a small chance of winning.

Cut the Pot   To take a percentage from each pot. Also called the "rake." This is how the casino makes money from a poker game.

Dead Hand   A hand that cannot continue to play because of an irregularity. A player's hand is declared dead if he is not at the table when the action is on him.

Dead Man's Hand   Aces and eights, so called because this is the hand that Wild Bill Hickok was holding when he was shot to death at a poker table in Deadwood, North Dakota.

Dead Money   Money in the pot that has been put there by players who have already folded their hand.

Deuce   The two card.

Dog   Shortened form of "underdog."

Dominated Hands   A hand that will usually lose to a better hand that people commonly play. For example, A,5 is dominated by A,Q. Consistently playing dominated hands is a certain way to lose money.

Double Belly Buster.   See *Belly Buster.*

Doyle (Texas Dolly) Brunson (the Man and the Hand)   A poker legend, author of a book many consider poker's Bible, and two-time winner of the World Series of Poker. The hand T,2 is called a "Doyle Brunson" because Doyle won successive world championships holding this hand. Whenever you see it, do what I am certain Doyle does with it 99 percent of the time: muck it without a second thought. It is a true garbage hand.

Draw   A hand that is not yet a good hand but may become one if the right cards fall. You may be drawing to a straight or a flush.

Drawing Dead   Drawing to a hand that even when made will not win the pot. If you are drawing to a straight when your opponent has a flush, for example, you are said to be drawing dead.

Draw Out   To make a drawing hand to beat an opponent who was beating you before the draw. You have "drawn out" on the other player.

Early Position   The next three seats after the Big Blind.

Effective Odds   The ratio between what you expect to win, if you make your hand, and the sum total of the bets you will have to call from the present round of betting to the end of the hand.

Equity   This is a somewhat controversial term. Some poker theorists use this term to refer to the value of a particular hand or combination of cards. More commonly it refers to your "share" of the pot in relation to how much is in the pot and your chances of winning it. So if there is $120 in the pot and you have a 50 percent chance of winning, you could be said to have $60 equity in the pot. I personally question the value of such a term as you will go on to win the pot or win nothing. Personally, I believe that this notion of pot equity causes players to make questionable decisions.

Expectation   Over the long run every hand can be said to have a positive or negative expectation, that is, the average profit or loss it will show over time. Ideally, one should never play hands that have an overall negative expectation. Of course, in the short run, even the worst hand can win a pot if the board cards favor it. Expectation also refers to the overall win rate if you make a certain play. For example, you may bluff three times and fail twice, but if the one time your bluff succeeds, you win more than the combined total of your three bets—your play has a positive expectation. The win rate can also be expressed as an expectation, which is the average hourly rate you expect to win over the long haul. The actual wins and losses in a single session can fluctuate widely, however.

Extra Blinds   When a new player enters a game, he usually has to put up an amount equal to the Big Blind. He "posts" a blind, and this is sometimes called an "extra blind." There may be more than one extra blind if more than one new player enters the game.

Family Pot   If all or almost all the players call before the Flop, this is called a "family pot."

Fast   Yes, I know you know what fast means, but in poker to play fast does not mean to play quickly! It means to play a hand aggressively, usually betting and raising as much as possible. You typically play fast when you have a good but not unbeatable hand and you do not want to give drawing hands a chance to catch up.

Favorite   The hand that has the best chance of winning before all the cards are dealt.

Fifth Street   An alternative name for the last community card or River card in Hold'em. Stud players sometimes use this term.

Fill   To draw a card to make a hand. If the board pairs to make your set a full house, your hand has been "filled up."

Fish   A weak, aimless player.

Flat Call   To call a bet without raising.

Flop   The first three simultaneously dealt and exposed community cards. Flop is also used as a verb, for example, "I flopped two pair."

Flush   Five cards of the same suit.

Fold   To drop out of a hand and not call a bet or raise.

Four Flush   Four cards to a flush

Four of a Kind   Four cards of the same rank.

Fourth Street   An alternative name for the Turn card.

Free Card   A Turn or River card that you get without having to call a bet. Sometimes a raise on the Flop is made in the hope that every player checks to you on the next round and thus gives you a free card. This is especially valuable if you are drawing to a hand.

Free Roll   A situation where two players have the same hand, but one has a chance to make a better hand. For example, two players both hold a pair of aces before the Flop. If the Flop comes down with three suited cards, the player holding the ace of that suit will be said to have a free roll on his opponent. He cannot lose the hand, but if another card of the same suit appears on the Turn or River, he can win the whole pot. Sometimes casinos offer free tournaments as a promotion and these are sometimes called "free roll tournaments."

Full House   Three cards of one rank and two of another. Three aces and two kings would be called "aces over kings."

Gut Shot   A draw to an inside straight. Also called a "belly buster."

Heads Up   To play against a single opponent. Some players specialize in this type of play, but most low-limit players have no clue how to play heads up. Avoid it until you are much better. You can lose a lot—fast—if you do not know what you are doing and even if you do!

Hit   When the Flop "hits" you, it contains cards that help your hand.

Hourly Rate   The amount of money a player expects to win on average. This average rate comes in big fits and starts. It is easily possible to win or lose forty times your hourly rate in a single session, even if overall you are a winning player.

House   The casino or card room that runs the game. The house make its money by collecting a time charge or by taking a small sum, or rake, from each pot.

Implied Odds Pot odds that do not currently exist, but may be included in your calculation based upon bets you expect to win if you make your hand. It is this consideration that sometimes allows you to make a call, even though strictly speaking the pot is not offering you the proper odds.

Inside Straight A straight that can only be made with a card of one rank. For example, if you had ace, king, and the Flop was 9,10,J, only a queen could give you a straight.

Jackpot One of the rare instances in poker when losing is better than winning! A jackpot is a form of special promotion now offered widely by casinos and card rooms in which a special bonus is paid to a player whose very good hand gets beaten by an even better hand. This is sometimes called a "bad beat jackpot." Jackpots can be over $100,000 in large and online casinos. They are funded by the house taking a small rake from each pot. While jackpots may encourage some players to enter the game, many have criticized them. First, because they lower the amount one can win from a pot, but also because jackpot money is often lost to the game forever. This is because when players win single large sums, they are more likely to use it to pay bills, mortgages, buy houses, cars, or boats, take vacations, and not put it back in the game. This means that there is less money around for winning players to win. Jackpots are good for realtors, car and boat dealers, and credit card companies.

Kicker An unpaired card used to determine the better hand of two equally ranked hands. For example, if, when all the cards are dealt, the top hand is a pair of aces. A player holding A,K will win over a player having A,Q, assuming that the pair of aces is the best hand. The player with the A,Q has been "out kicked" by the player holding the king.

Late Position A position in the round of betting in which you act after most of the other players. Usually the button and one to the right of the button.

Legitimate Hand   A hand with true value, not a bluffing hand.

Limit   The predetermined amount that a player may bet on any round of betting.

Limp In   When a player calls rather than raises on the first round of betting, he is said to have limped in.

Live One   A bad, loose player who loses a lot of money.

Lock   A lock is a hand guaranteed to win at least part of the pot. (See also *Nuts*).

Loose   Playing loose simply means playing more hands than optimum and holding on to them for a longer time. A loose table is a table with many loose players. Most low-limit players are loose players. Loose isn't always bad—excessively tight play can be equally costly, especially at high levels of play. A loose call is a borderline, inadvisable, or even incorrect call.

   For example, "He was playing so loose, it seemed like he was playing every hand he was dealt."

Main Pot   When a player goes all-in in a table-stakes game, that player is only eligible to win the main pot—the pot consisting of those bets he was able to match. Additional bets are then placed in a side pot by the dealers and are contested among the remaining players.

Make   To make a hand means to get a decent hand that has a shot at winning the pot.

Maniac   A player who plays extremely loosely and aggressively, often betting, raising, and re-raising with poor cards in poor situations. Maniacs at the table tend to increase the fluctuations in your bankroll considerably. Please refer to the book or DVD set for what to do when a maniac is at the table.

Middle Pair   If there are three cards of different ranks on the Flop, and you pair the middle one, you have middle pair.

Middle Position   The fourth, fifth, and sixth seats to the left of the big blind.

Miss   When the Flop contains no cards that help your hand.

Monster   An extremely strong hand, one that is almost certain to win the pot.

Muck   The pile of discarded cards in front of the dealer, or the act of putting cards in this pile, and therefore taking them out of play. The common house rule is that as soon as the cards touch the muck, they are ineligible to win the pot.

No Limit   As you might guess, any game in which there is no limit on the sizes of bets and raises. All the major tournaments have a no-limit Hold'em game as their premier game. The World Series of Poker is a no-limit Hold'em tournament. Note that in table-stakes games, players are still limited to the amount of money they have in front of them.

Nuts (or **Nut)**   This is the best possible hand. In Hold'em, the nuts can never be less than trips. "Nut xxx" is sometimes used to refer to the best hand of a particular type, especially a straight or flush. You must learn to quickly recognize what the nuts is for any given board in Hold'em.

Odds   A ratio of two probabilities, usually the probability of making a hand to the probability of not making the hand. Thus, if you have a 25 percent chance of making a hand, the odds are 3 to 1 against you making it. In poker, this is especially important in considering pot odds.

Off-Suit   Not of the same suit. Sometimes abbreviated to just "off." For example, "I'll play K,10 off-suit occasionally, but only in late position if there has been no raise."

One-Gap   See *Inside Straight*.

Open   To open, or open betting, is to make the first bet in a betting round. For example: "I opened with a small pair in late position hoping to make a set on the Flop."

Open-Ended Straight (Draw) A straight draw is open-ended if it consists of four consecutive cards (none of them an ace). The straight can be completed at either end. (See also *Belly Buster* and *Inside Straight*.)

Open-Ender See *Open-Ended Straight*.

Option When a player posts a live blind, as he first sits down or after he has been away from the table for a long time, that player is given the option to raise when the action is on him, even if no one else has raised. The dealer will typically say something such as "your option" to remind him.

Out An out is a card that will improve your hand, usually one that you think will make it a winner. In Hold'em, an open-ended straight draw has eight outs (the four cards of each rank will complete the straight). But it may be only six outs if there are two suited cards on the table and someone else is drawing for the flush.

Outdraw To make a better hand than an opponent by merit of the cards you draw.

Over Button In some games, players can take "over" buttons, which means they are willing to play at higher limits. Any time everyone left in the hand has an over button, the limits go up.

Overcall Any additional call after a bet is first called. For example, player A bets, player B calls, and player C overcalls.

Overcard A card higher than the highest card on the board. If you hold K,J and the flop is J,9,5, you have top pair with an overcard. If the flop is 10,9,2, you just have two overcards.

Overpair A pocket pair higher than the highest card on the board. If you hold K,K and the flop is Q,5, you have an overpair.

Paint   A jack, king, or queen (a card with painted picture on it).

Pair   Two cards of the same rank. If you hold A,A, you have a pair.

Pass   To fold.

Passive   Passive is a style of play that is characterized by reluctance to bet and raise. This does not mean tight play. A typical loose-passive player will call with almost anything, but raise with only very powerful hands (see *Calling Station*). A passive table is one with many passive players, so that, for example, few hands are raised before the Flop.

Pay Off   To call a bet by a player you're reasonably sure has you beaten. Weak players pay you off more often than strong players. This makes for a profitable game.

Perfect   When you only have one way to make a hand. If you hold 9,J, you need three perfect cards 8,T,Q for the nut straight. To "catch perfect" is to hit perfect cards.

Play   To play a hand in poker means to make it past the first round of betting.

In Hold'em, this means calling the Big Blind. If someone says he hasn't played a hand in hours, he is complaining that he hasn't had cards good enough to play.

To make a play or put a play on someone means to present a pattern of behavior inconsistent with your cards that will mislead your opponents and cause them to make a mistake. This could mean bluffing them out of a pot, but it can also mean getting them to call when you have a strong hand, or more generally anything (legitimate) intended to manipulate their behavior to cause them to make errors.

Play Back   To play back at someone is to raise his opening bet or to re-raise his raise.

Play the Board   In Hold'em, if your best five-card hand uses the five community cards, you are said to be playing the board. The best you can do in this situation is to split the pot with anyone who calls. If you are sure the board cannot be improved, you should bet, as very poor players who misread the board may fold.

Pocket   The two cards dealt to you face down or the first two face down are called your pocket cards.

Pocket Pair   Two pocket cards of the same rank.

Poker   Poker refers to a number of card games. This book is about the most popular form, Texas Hold'em. A majority of poker games do share some common features, especially betting in rounds and the ranking of hands. The varieties played in home games probably number in the thousands. Some common public card room games include Texas Hold'em, Seven-Card Stud, and Omaha.

Position   Position refers to your place at the table, in relation to the nominal dealer, and defines the order of betting within a particular betting round. The first few players to act are said to be in early position, the next few in middle position, and the last few in late position. Late position is best, because you have the advantage of knowing what your opponents have done. You can play more hands from later positions. In Hold'em, position is fixed from one round of betting to the next, and the dealer, the player on the Button, is always in last position and is last to act in all but the first round of betting, when the Big Blinds act first.

   More generally, to have position on someone is to be in a position to bet after him, either during a particular hand or in general. You have position on anyone sitting immediately to your right, because you will usually be able to act after him.

Position Bet   A position bet is a bet made more on the strength of one's position than solely on the strength of one's hand. A player on the button in Hold'em is in good position to "steal" the blinds if no one else opens the betting.

Post   To post a bet is to place your chips in the pot (or, commonly, out in front of you so that your bet can be counted). In poker, posting usually means a forced bet, such as posting the Big Blind, usually equivalent to one full first-round bet.

Pot   All the money in the middle of the poker table that goes to the winner of the hand is called the "pot." Any player who has not yet folded his hand is said to be "in the pot." A player who has called an initial bet is said to have entered the pot.

Pot Limit   Any game in which the maximum bet or raise is the size of the pot. For raises, the size of the pot includes the call, so if the pot is $100 and player A bets $100, player B can bet a total of $400 for a maximum raise, calling the $100 and then raising the size of the $300 pot.

Pot Odds   The ratio of the amount of money in the pot to the amount of money it will cost you to call a bet. The greater the pot odds, the more likely you should be to call because you will have to win fewer times over the long haul to make that a positive expectation.

Presto   A nickname for pocket fives. This nickname comes from the Internet newsgroup rec.gambling.poker (www.recpoker.com) and is sometimes used among the readership of that newsgroup to identify other members.

Prop   Short for proposition player. (See *Proposition Player*.)

Proposition Player   A proposition player, or prop, is a player who is paid by the house (casino) to play poker, usually to keep games going or to get games started. Props are paid a salary, but they gamble with their own money. Props either learn how to play pretty solid poker or they run out of money. (See also *Shill*.)

Protect   To protect a hand (usually a made hand) is to bet to lessen the chances of anyone outdrawing you by inducing them to fold an inferior hand or a drawing hand. A hand that needs protection is one that is almost certainly best right now, but that is vulnerable to being outdrawn. Large pots make it difficult to protect hands, especially in limit poker where the bet size is pre-determined, because players will be willing to chase more long shots, as the pot is often offering them the correct odds or close to the correct odds. The structure of a game has a large impact on how easy it is to protect a hand, as do the personalities of the players at the table. It's easiest to protect a hand in no-limit Hold'em play, where you can make it as expensive as your chip stack allows for someone to draw to a hand. To protect your cards is also to place a chip or some other small object (such objects vary widely from the quaint to the downright bizarre) on top of them so that they aren't accidentally mucked by the dealer, mixed with another player's discarded cards, or otherwise become dead.

Provider   A provider is a poker player who makes the game profitable for the other players at the table. Similar in meaning to fish (no, not the type in your local aquarium, but the aimless players found in some games), although the provider has a somewhat less negative connotation. A provider might be a decent player who just happens to be playing out of his league. He provides for the better players, probably something he does not really intend to do!

Push   What the dealer does with the pot when he figures out who the winner is. He pushes it to the winner!

Put On   To put someone on a hand is to guess what he is holding.

Quads Four of a kind.

Rabbit Hunting Rabbit hunting is the act of asking to see what cards would have come up if a hand had continued. It also means rifling through the muck and is usually illegal in most card rooms.

Rack Most usually the plastic racks that hold 100 chips in 5 stacks of 20. If someone asks for a rack, it usually means he is about to leave the table. Someone is said to be "racking up" a game if he is winning a lot of money at the table. In most card rooms, you cannot place chips in a rack on the table. In one card room I played in where this rule was not in force, an attractive woman was doing well and had placed about $1,000 of chips in two racks on the table. One new, slightly inebriated player upon joining the game stared at the chips and then blurted out in admiration, "Nice rack!" She was not amused, but I still believe he meant the chips.

Rag A card, usually a low card, that, when it appears, has no apparent effect on the hand. A flop of 9,6,3 is a rag flop—few playable hands match the flop well. If the table shows K,Q,J,T, all of diamonds, a deuce of hearts on the River is a rag.

Rail The rail is the sideline at a poker table separating spectators from the field of play. Watching from the rail means watching a poker game as a spectator. People on the rail are sometimes called "railbirds."

Railbird Someone watching a game from the rail.

Rainbow Three cards of different suits, usually on the Flop.

Raise After someone has opened the betting in a round, a player can increase, or raise, the amount of the bet. For example, if the betting limit is $5 and player A bets $5, player B can fold, call the $5, or raise it to $10.

Rake The money removed from each pot by the house. Medium-

and higher-limit games typically have a time charge rather than a rake. A typical Atlantic City low-limit rake is 10 percent of the pot up to a $4 maximum. An excessive rake can make a game unprofitable, even for good players. Generally speaking, one must play a shade tighter in pot-raked games.

Rank Each card has a suit and a rank. The ten of diamonds and the ten of spades have the same rank. A pair is two cards of the same rank.

Read To read someone is to have a good idea from his play (or through tells) what his cards might be. To have a read on someone is to have a good understanding of how he plays.

Redraw A way to further improve your hand after hitting a draw is a redraw. For example, if you hold 10♦, 9♦, and the Flop is J♦, Q♦, 3♣, you have a flush draw. If the Turn is the ace of diamonds, you have made your flush and picked up an inside straight flush redraw.

Represent To bet or raise in such a way as to indicate that you have a certain hand. For instance, when you bet or raise after the third suited card hits the board, you are representing a flush, even if you don't actually have one.

Re-raise Any raise after the first raise in a round. For example, player A bets, player B raises, and player C (or A) re-raises.

Ring Game Poker played for cash. The term *ring game* is used to differentiate such games from tournaments.

River The last of the five community cards that make up the board. Sometimes called "fifth street."

Rock A player who plays extremely tight is a rock. Many retirees play like this. Rocks don't create a lot of action, but when they enter a pot, more often than not they're in as a favorite. This is a winning strategy at some tables, especially at a table full of very loose players, but it makes them very predictable. Players with more varied strategies will generally beat them handily.

Rock Garden   A table populated with rocks.

Rockets   Or "pocket rockets"—a pair of aces Pre-Flop.

Round   A round can refer either to a round of betting or a round of hands. A betting round usually begins after a card or several cards are dealt. Each player is given a chance to act, and the round ends when everyone has either folded or called the last bet or raise. Each round of betting is followed either by further dealing or by a showdown of cards. A round of hands consists of one hand dealt by each player at the table (or, when there is a house dealer, one hand with the dealer button at each position). In a round of Hold'em, you're in each position once.

Royal Straight Flush   An ace-high straight flush is a royal straight flush, a royal flush, or just a royal. It's the best hand in poker, played for high.

Runner-Runner   A hand made on the last two cards. (See also *Backdoor.*)

Rush   A player who wins a large number of pots in a short period is said to be on a rush. Some players superstitiously feel that a rush is an independent entity and will "play their rush" or "bet their rush" after winning a few pots—that is, play looser and more aggressively, or just be certain to play out each hand until the rush ends. Personally, I have always believed that the rush is a fallacy. Cards have no memory.

Sandbag   Sandbagging usually means check-raising. Sandbagging sometimes means concealing your strength for the purpose of increasing your profit. Slow playing is sometimes described as sandbagging. Check-raising or slowplaying, despite this derogatory nickname, are not unethical and are only considered such by the lamebrained.

Scare Card   A card that when it appears makes a better hand more likely. In Hold'em, a third suited card on the River is a scare card, because it makes a flush possible. Scare cards will often make it difficult for the best hand to bet and also offer a bluffing opportunity.

Seat Charge   See *Time Charge.*

Seating List   In most casino card rooms, if there is no seat available for you when you arrive, you can put your name on a list to be seated when a seat becomes available. Typically, games are listed across the top of a board, and names are written below each game so that players are seated for games in the order in which they arrive.

Second Pair   Same as middle pair. (See *Middle Pair.*)

See   To call a bet is sometimes referred to as seeing it. Avoid saying this in casinos, despite what you may have seen in the movies. If you say, "I'll see you and raise," it will probably be called a string bet. (See *String Bet.*)

Semi-bluff   A bluff with a hand that is almost certainly second best now but may become the best hand if the right cards fall. The power of this play is that it can win three ways: by in fact being the best hand, by becoming the best hand, or by causing others to fold.

Set   When you have a pocket pair and a third card of the rank appears on the board, you have a set. (See *Trips.*)

Seven-Card Stud   Of the poker games most commonly played in public card rooms, Seven-Card Stud is second only in popularity to Hold'em. In Seven-Card Stud (sometimes Seven Stud or just Stud), each player is dealt seven cards: two down, then four up, and a final card down. There is a round of betting after the first up card and after each subsequent card dealt. Stud is usually played with a small ante and a forced bet called a "bring in" on third street. In limit games, the bet size typically increases on fifth street.

Shill   A shill is similar to a proposition player except a shill gambles with the card room's money instead of his own. (See *Proposition Player*.)

Shootout   A tournament format in which a single player ends up with the entire prize money or in which play continues at each table until only one player remains.

Shorthanded   A game is said to be shorthanded when it falls below a certain number of players. In Hold'em, any game with five players or less is generally called shorthanded. Because the number of players at a table has a significant impact on strategy, learning to play well shorthanded is an important skill. Avoid shorthanded play if you are a novice. It can be costly.

Short Stack   A short stack is a stack that's too small to cover the likely betting in a hand. A player who has such a stack is said to be short-stacked.

Showdown   When all the betting is done, if more than one player is still in the pot, the showdown is the process of showing cards to determine who wins the pot. The last player to bet or raise is required to show his cards first, and any player can ask to see the hands of any callers at the showdown.

Show One, Show All   A common card room rule that states that if a player shows his cards to anyone at the table, he can be asked to show everyone else (even if the player would ordinarily not be required to show his hand). This usually comes up at the end of a hand that did not reach showdown. Obviously, showing one's hand to someone else who has cards is illegal.

Shuffle   Before each hand, the dealer shuffles the cards—that is, mixes them up to make their order as unpredictable as possible. Most casinos have fairly specific requirements for how the cards are to be shuffled.

Side Pot   See *Main Pot*.

Slowplay   To slowplay is to underbet a very strong hand. The purpose of slowplaying a hand is to give other players the chance to make stronger second-best hands and also to conceal the strength of your hand. Instead of betting early and risking the loss of future action, slowplay means checking and calling. It is of course best to slowplay when you have a hand that no one is likely to actually catch (e.g., four of a kind).

   Most players slowplay far too much and then complain about getting outdrawn.

Slowroll   To reveal one's hand slowly at showdown, often one card at a time, is to slowroll anyone else who thinks the pot might be theirs. This is usually only done with a winning hand, for the purpose of irritating other players. It is very bad poker manners, so don't do it.

Small Blind   The smaller of the two forced bets in Hold'em. The Small Blind is immediately to the left of the Button and is first to act (in worst position) in all betting rounds except the Pre-Flop.

Smooth Call   A type of slowplaying. To call one or more bets with a hand would usually be raised with the intention of trapping players in later rounds.

Snap Off   To beat someone, often a bluffer, and usually without an especially powerful hand is to snap him off.

Speed   Speed refers to the level of aggression. Fast play is more aggressive, slow play (not slowplaying) is more passive. Good players may change speeds to disguise their play.

Speeding   Someone who is caught bluffing is sometimes said to be caught speeding.

Splash (the Pot)   To throw your chips into the pot, instead of placing them in front of you, is to splash the pot. Doing so annoys dealers, because it can make it difficult for the dealer to determine if you have bet the correct amount or to keep track of the action.

Split Pot   A hand in which two players showdown the same hand results in a pot split between those two players.

Spread   When a card room starts a table for a particular game, it is said to spread that game.

Spread Limit   Betting limits in which there is a fixed minimum and maximum bet for each betting round, and any amount in between these limits may be bet.

Stack   The amount of money you have in front of you on the poker table.

Steal   To (attempt to) steal a pot is to make a bet when it appears no one else has anything. Stealing blinds is often done from late position.

Steam   A player who is on tilt is sometimes said to be steaming. A steam raise is a raise made more out of frustration than out of strategic concerns. Steaming is a bad idea, but can be hard to avoid.

Straddle   The player immediately to the left of the Small Blind may raise before looking at his cards, effectively posting an additional blind bet. This is called a "straddle" or "live straddle." House rules often make these bets live so that the player who posts a live straddle has the option of raising when it's his turn again even if no one has re-raised. Straddling is a pretty dumb idea. Never do it.

Straight   A hand composed of five cards of consecutive ranks (aces count as high or low). The hand 2,3,4,5,6 is a six-high straight, or a straight to the six. 7,8,9,T,J is a jack-high straight, or a straight to the jack. In comparing straights, the straight to the higher card wins.

Straight Flush   A hand consisting of five cards of consecutive ranks of the same suit. A straight flush is the strongest possible hand. Of two straight flushes, the one with the highest high card is better. An ace-high straight flush is often called a royal flush, a royal straight flush, or just a royal.

Street   The cards that come out one at a time in a card game are sometimes referred to as different numbered streets. In Hold'em, players sometimes refer to the Turn and River as fourth and fifth street.

String Bet   Most casinos require you to make your entire bet at once. In other words, you can't raise by putting out enough to call and then reaching back to your stack for your raise. Also, because verbal statements are considered binding at most poker games, if you say, "I call your bet and raise you ten more," you have called, because the raise was added afterward. To be on the safe side, when you want to raise, it's best to say "raise" so that your bet won't be mistaken. The reason for the string bet rule is to prevent players from unfairly misleading other players about the size of their bet. By the way, when it comes to betting, the movies mostly have it wrong.

Structure   The structure of a game refers to the details about the betting, blinds, and what may be bet on any round. In card rooms, games are typically posted along with shorthand for the limits. For example, $5–$10 Hold'em is usually a fixed-limit game, played with $5 bets and raises Pre-Flop and on the Flop, and $10 bets and raises on the Turn and the River. Spread-limit games are ones in which the betting in a given round is constrained to a particular range. So a $1–$4 spread-limit game would allow a bet from $1 to $4 on any round. The structure of a game has a substantial impact on appropriate strategy.

Stuck   Losing money.

Stud   Usually short for Seven-Card Stud. Also refers to Stud games in general, including Five-Card Stud, in which each player is dealt a number of nonshared cards and must use only those cards.

Suck Out   To win a hand by virtue of hitting a very weak draw, often with poor pot odds.

Suit   Clubs, diamonds, hearts, and spades. Also, something they insist men wear in very fancy foreign casinos.

Suited   Of the same suit. Also, men wearing the right clothing in very fancy foreign casinos.

Sweat   To sweat someone is to watch him play from the rail to lend your support.

Table   The word *table* can be used to refer to community cards, the poker table itself, or the players at the table as a group.
Examples: "When the ace hit the table, I checked."
"The table was playing loose, so I was bluffing less than usual."
"This is a nice table, I especially like the tartan finish."

Table Change   If you're playing at a public card room and you'd like to play at a table other than the one you're currently at, you can ask the floor staff for a table change. Various card rooms handle this differently, but typically you'll be moved as soon as an opening develops, and a player from the seating list will be moved into your seat.

Table Cop   A player who calls with the intention of keeping other players honest is said to be playing table cop. Also a player who makes an effort to point out violations often of insignificant casino rules. The latter can be very annoying.

Table Stakes   Table stakes is simply the rule that a player may only wager money he has on the table at the beginning of a hand. Almost all poker games are played this way. Usually, it also implies that money may not be removed from the table at any time (exceptions are made for tipping), although money may be added to one's stacks between hands. A player who goes all-in at a table stakes game may not continue to bet and only competes for the main pot. To the best of my knowledge, Maryland is the only place where most of the games are not table stakes. They also talk funny in Maryland.

Table Talk   Any discussion at the table of the hand currently underway, especially by players not involved in the pot and especially any talk that might affect play. Depending on the nature of the discussion, table talk is often considered somewhere between rude and an act of war. The most common example of table talk to be avoided is announcing what cards you've folded. In England, table talk may get you banned from the card room. Don't talk about hands unless you are in them, and don't suggest plays during a hand to other players when you're not in a pot.

Tell   A tell is any habit or behavior that gives other players more information about your hand than they would have simply from your play. For instance, you might unconsciously scratch your ear every time you bluff. Or you might notice that another player's hands shake whenever he has a strong hand. The value of tells in the low-limit game is highly overrated. In high-limit poker they may be invaluable.

Texas Hold'em   Hey, guys, read the book for pity's sake!

Three of a kind   Three cards of the same rank. Also called "trips."

Tight   Playing tight simply means playing fewer hands and folding them earlier. A tight table is a table dominated by tight players. Most players at low-limits do not play tightly enough, but tight play alone (without suitable aggression) will not make you into a winning player.

Tilt   Good poker means disciplined play. However, even good players are often tempted to make dubious plays when they get frustrated, angry, or upset for any reason. They go "on tilt." I knew one player who did it every game. The rest of us would make side bets as to when during the evening he would begin throwing a tantrum. Tilt comes from the world of pinball when players try to tilt the machine to gain an advantage. Typical tilt play is too loose and aggressive because a player on tilt wants very badly to win a pot and isn't rational enough to wait for cards that are worth playing or situations that are worth attacking.

Time Charge   Money collected periodically from each player is called a "time charge" or a "seat charge," and you're said to be "paying time" to play. "Time" is also what you're supposed to say whenever you need more than about a second to decide what to do.

To Go   An amount "to go" is the amount it takes to enter the pot.

Toke   A tip, usually a tip to the dealer after winning the pot. Tips are usually between $1 and $5, depending on the limit, the size of the pot, and the generosity of the player.

Top Pair   If there are three cards of different ranks on the Flop, and you pair the highest one, you have top pair.

Tournament   The general idea behind poker tournaments is that a bunch of poker players sit down with the same number of chips (tournament chips) and eventually only one player has all the chips. The order in which players drop out decides who finishes where. To ensure that the event will finish in a reasonable time, tournaments institute a schedule by which the blinds increase. Tournaments are usually played with chips that have no value outside of the tournament. So a buy-in of $100 might get you $2,000 in tournament chips to play with, but you can't cash them out in the middle. Tournaments are varied, and you would be wise to read about them in a book that describes strategies and tactics for tournament play before playing in one.

Trey Threes are sometimes called "treys."

Trips Three of a kind.

Turn The fourth of five community cards in Hold'em.

Two Pair A hand consisting of two cards of one rank, and two cards of another rank (and an unpaired card).

Underdog When two hands face off, the underdog is the one who is less likely to win than the other. Surely you knew that, right?

Under the Gun The first player to act after the Blinds is said to be under the gun.

Up Aces up is two pair with aces as the higher pair. Kings up is two pair with kings as the higher pair. What do you think queens up is?

Value Value means the return you get on your investment; the expected increase in your equity in the pot (your return) as compared to the size of your bet or raise (your investment).

Variance If you have a sufficient advantage at the game you're playing, you expect to make money over the long haul. Variance is the statistical measure of dispersion, or just how widely your results will be distributed. When variance is high enough, a small advantage may be of no use during your life-time. When variance is low enough, a small sample will be much more likely to reflect your real advantage (or disadvantage). In other words, variance describes just how long the long haul is. In poker terms, high variance means that a small number of hands will not be very representative of your long-term expectation. Variance is such a strong contributor to poker results that it often obscures the importance of good play. The best player at the table may start with the best cards and still have far less than a 50 percent chance of winning the hand. A skilled professional can lose money over days or weeks without necessarily playing badly. Bad play may be rewarded in the short term. Or as one poker buddy once said to me in exasperation, "Randomness is a bitch ain't it?"

Variance is what makes losing players think they have a chance in the long run, and what gives them a real chance in the short run. It keeps poor players coming back. Different qualities of the other players at the table can contribute to your overall variance at a given table. If many of the players are maniacs, your variance may be high at that table. However, exceptionally weak and passive players will reduce your variance. The variance you experience will be affected not just by the nature of the game but also by your style of play and by the styles of those you play against.

Walk   To walk in poker is to be away from the table long enough to miss one or more hands. Such people and people who do so frequently are called walkers. Perhaps in Australian casinos they go on walkabout. Australian players, is this so?

Weak   A style of play characterized by a readiness to fold and a reluctance to raise. Weak is also used generally to describe a poor player or a table that's easy to beat. It has also been used to describe jokes I make at the table. Whoops, there's another one.

Wild Card   A card that can serve as any other card in making your hand. Casino poker does not have wild card games.

Index